D1569911

Trust

Trust

The Secret Weapon of Effective Business Leaders

Kathy Bloomgarden

St. Martin's Press ⚐ New York

www.stmartins.com

Design by Nancy Singer Olaguera

ISBN-13: 978-0-312-34984-4
ISBN-10: 0-312-34984-X

First Edition: February 2007

10 9 8 7 6 5 4 3 2 1

To my husband, Zach,

for all of his love, encouragement and patience,

and to

Rachel, Keith, Matthew, Bryan, Max, and Olivia.

Contents

Acknowledgments

THERE ARE NUMEROUS people I would like to thank for their encouragement and support. These include the many business leaders and clients who generously gave their time in person and on the phone: Daniel Vasella, Novartis; Ed Breen and Eric Pillmore, Tyco; Fred Hassan and Ken Banta, Schering-Plough; Arthur Sulzberger Jr., *The New York Times;* Bob Hormats, Goldman Sachs; Nick Butler and Lee Edwards, BP; Rhonda Seegal, Xerox; Dan Scheinman, Cisco; David Handler, UBS; Ben Heineman, GE; Carl Johnson, Campbells; Shelley Diamond, Young & Rubicam. They were open and honest, frankly expressing their beliefs, expounding on their values, and freely discussing challenges they had faced. It is their stories that are the foundation of this book.

Several people were important in providing research assistance, especially Nancy Shepherdson. Adam Snyder was an invaluable colleague, and his work on the drafts was critical to formulating the key themes of the book. Angela Spruill was outstanding in helping me keep the book organized and on schedule. My family, especially my husband, Zach, reviewed drafts and gave me great feedback. My brother, Peter Finn, first suggested that I consider writing this book, and my father, David Finn, has, throughout my life, emphasized the importance of values in business.

Finally, I would like to thank Linda Konner for introducing me to the wonderful St. Martin's team and especially my editor, Phil Revzin, whose sharp pen and keen mind contributed tremendously to the text.

I am grateful to all for their input and guidance.

Introduction

IT HAS BECOME almost impossible to avoid news stories about the wrongdoing and greed of CEOs and their top teams. While the business people I work with every day are far different from the ill-intentioned business executive often portrayed in the media, these reports of malfeasance have clearly had an impact. The public's confidence in business is extremely low, the tenure of CEOs is shrinking, and global companies have become the least trusted of institutions.

But I see something else happening in the business world that is not being reported. Trust building, ethics, responsibility—what people in business once thought of as soft management skills—are on the minds of top managers and are becoming foundations of strong leadership. The autocratic chieftain whose command-and-control style conveyed that rules are more important than innovation and that ideas from below are not likely to be valued is no longer effective in this era of powerful stakeholders and information flowing at lightning speed. Today's top executives operate in a world far more transparent than ever before, where every move is scrutinized and leadership skills are constantly tested. In this new world of instant communications many groups have strong opinions about what a business is doing right, and wrong. Each of these stakeholders—investors, employees, customers, policymakers, and nongovernmental organizations (NGOs)—voice their concerns openly and aggressively, often seeking to make those in charge uncomfortable. This adds volatility to the normal rhythm of business. Short-term performance flaws are magnified, mistakes become highly visible, and there is strong pressure to promptly air any difficulties that arise.

This new environment has created an opportunity for those leaders who can gain the trust of their stakeholders. As chief executive officer of Ruder Finn Inc., one of the world's largest independent public relations firms, I have worked with many successful CEOs who understand that trust can drive success. My observations led me to realize that certain aspects of CEO behavior go a long way toward explaining why some can lead their companies to often surprising heights of success. I also began to understand that the characteristics they share can be applied by any leader, whether a corporate CEO, an executive of a not-for-profit organization, a politician, a division president, or even an ambitious young person at the beginning of his or her career. These drivers of trust are not inborn. They are acquired. They can be learned and strengthened by any executive who wishes to become more effective. While most of the corporate leaders profiled in this book are CEOs, the lessons are equally valid for those responsible for any kind of organization.

Most corporate leaders are neither heroes nor villains. They are human beings trying to do the best job possible. Yet there are some leaders who stand out for their ability to cope with whatever is thrown at them, and emerge stronger. These leaders have a different strategic vision about their job, one that is rooted in today's fast-paced information environment. They are unfazed by the day-to-day events swirling around them. Instead, they lead according to an inner conviction and a long-term vision that is genuine because it fits their personality. They are mindful of what is really important to the diverse audiences to whom they are responsible and, as a result, build strong companies that are rewarded by the marketplace over the long term. They possess a certain boldness—a belief in themselves and a profound understanding of their stakeholders that allows them to set a course early in their tenure and sustain it over time. These leaders have something to teach us about surviving and thriving in the face of increasing challenges. They take independent thinking to a new level, refusing to be thrown off course by outside pressures, short-term results, or the demands of Wall Street. They are not driven by compensation. Despite considerable press coverage of CEO salaries and compensation packages, money is not what inspires the most successful corporate chieftains. Having more money has little to do with the drive to do something useful with our lives. The best leaders accomplish their goals by inspiring their companies to reach new heights of success and meaning, and by fulfilling their responsibilities to multiple groups.

People argue whether the charismatic CEO or the low-key CEO is right for our times, but that's not the right question. We all operate in a world of full disclosure, and business leaders have to be transparent as well. Successful leaders who add the most value to their companies tend to make decisions not based on short-term financial goals, but on strongly held values. They develop a reservoir of trust among all their key stakeholders because they are sensitive to what is in the long-term best interest of the company, and the world.

Some stakeholders may discover that they disagree with a leader's values, and will either leave the company or become forceful critics. Most of us, though, share certain ideas about a clean environment, safe places for our children to grow up, curing diseases, and the importance of basic human rights. Those beliefs can guide our actions and complement our leadership styles.

It would be naive to think that any leader can thrive for long without successful financial performance. But a results orientation is only one important driver of success. Leaders who understand that their duty to their stakeholders goes beyond revenue and strong profit numbers will, I believe, be out in front of the pack, gaining cooperation and support as they navigate around the inevitable pitfalls that beset all companies.

Throughout this book, leaders will be profiled who display the best of these trust-inspiring behaviors. It is not necessary to practice all of them—or even practice one of them perfectly—in order to enhance success and staying power. Rather, a portfolio of strategies and responsibilities will be presented aimed at strengthening relationships in ways that achieve connectivity and trust. The stories are either inspiring or cautionary. Sometimes they are both. In all cases they demonstrate a new way of dealing with tough problems while sustaining trust.

Some of those profiled in the following pages have been my clients for many years. Others I met for the first time while writing this book. I hope all provide insights about how top managers cope with tough challenges.

Following the trust-building strategies outlined in this book does not mean you will not run into difficulties. It doesn't even mean you will become bulletproof, or will never be removed from office. It certainly doesn't mean you will not be criticized as leaders of *The New York Times*, BP, and others have experienced. Every business goes through highs and lows, and every human makes mistakes. Yet my experience working with top executives at companies all over the world has revealed a common denominator of success. Leaders who concentrate on building and sustaining the trust of their stakeholders will have a greater chance to gain the flexibility they need to achieve their strategic, performance, and personal goals.

Trust

1

Trusted Leadership as an Imperative for Success

The price of greatness is responsibility.
Winston S. Churchill[1]

THE GIANT MULTINATIONAL pharmaceuticals company Novartis SA contributes more than 2 percent of its annual sales—in 2005 $696 million—to its Access to Medicine program, which gives away drugs to those most in need around the world. The program has cured more than 5.5 million patients of leprosy, treated more than 3 million malaria sufferers, and provided more than half a million free treatments for tuberculosis. "As leaders, we are responsible for setting an example through our actions," says Novartis CEO Daniel Vasella.

WHEN ED BREEN became chairman and CEO of Tyco International after Dennis Koslowski left under a cloud of suspicion, investors adopted a wait-and-see attitude. But their patience wouldn't have lasted long had Breen not stepped forward almost immediately with a solid hundred-day plan.

Breen told investors that he was:

1. Committed to integrity
2. Dedicated to strong corporate governance
3. Focused on customer satisfaction

4. Intent on strengthening leadership in subsidiary companies
5. Devoted to creating a positive environment for employees

Breen's stated goals were reinforced by his behavior. During his first hundred days he fired the board, hired a senior vice president of corporate governance, rebuilt every senior corporate direct report, devised a new operating blueprint, and put everything under a Six Sigma umbrella. The result was an entirely new corporate culture and a rebuilt internal trust. That's the kind of affirmative action Wall Street recognizes and usually rewards.

WHEN ANNE MULCAHY became president of Xerox in 2000 the company was facing a looming liquidity crisis. She boldly announced that Xerox had "an unsustainable business model" and would have to undergo a dramatic, transformational shift. The stock price almost immediately plunged 26 percent. But Mulcahy realized that as the top executive driving a sharp turn, her most critical job was to be brutally honest to those outside and inside the company about Xerox's near-term future. She realized the urgency and the need to motivate Xerox's employees. In twelve months she traveled 100,000 miles talking to employees about the new direction she wanted to take the company. The stock price tripled between December 2000 and February 2006.

In 1997 Sir John Browne, group chief executive at BP (formerly British Petroleum), stood before an audience of fellow executives at Stanford Business School and pledged to cut carbon dioxide emissions by 10 percent in five years in order to combat global warming. At the time, most of the business world—and certainly the other oil industry leaders—weren't even admitting that global warming was a serious problem. Soon afterward BP launched its new green sunburst logo with an ad campaign aimed at signaling that the oil business as usual was a thing of the past at BP. Browne began talking about earning a seat at someone else's table, not just allowing critics to sit at his table.

• • •

THE FOUR DISPARATE CEOs mentioned above, whom we'll meet in detail later, share a common characteristic: They have all made earning the trust of stakeholders the cornerstone of building their companies' bottom lines. Once ubiquitous, such leaders are only now coming back to the forefront of international business.

It wasn't long ago that the vast majority of corporate leaders were heroes, lionized in the press, on television, and in boardrooms, even leaders of unprofitable companies were looked to as sources of wisdom and enlightenment. No longer. In the wake of the indictments and convictions of former top executives at WorldCom, Adelphia, Tyco, Enron, and elsewhere, even the best news from the corporate arena is subjected to intense scrutiny.

Corporate decisions are questioned everywhere, from the halls of Congress and city councils to annual meetings to the blogs. Shareholders, whom you might expect would want companies to do everything possible to make high profits, are increasingly reading between the numbers and questioning the reality behind them. The corporate scandals of the recent past have taught them that they too can be fooled.

The misdeeds of a handful of top executives have done serious damage to the institution of the CEO and have exacerbated the pressures on all executives. Lack of trust has eroded the goodwill and respect they previously counted on in doing their jobs. All companies have suffered from this bad behavior. According to a 2004 Gallup poll, only about 20 percent of the American public rated business executives as "high" or "very high" in honesty. Only lawyers and car salesmen ranked lower.[2]

Corporations are perceived equally poorly. According to the international survey firm Globescan Inc., only 38 percent of people around the world trust that global companies will operate in the best interests of society, compared with 68 percent who feel this way about NGOs, also known as nonprofit organizations.[3] Clearly, business leaders are perceived to be operating without a strong set of values.

Low Confidence in Business Leaders

How would you rate the honesty and ethical standards of people in these fields?[1]
Percent saying "high" or "very high"

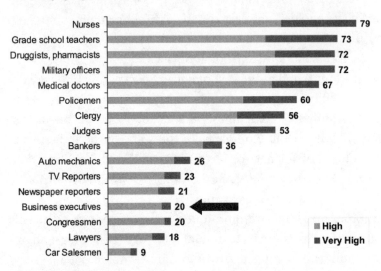

Field	Percent
Nurses	79
Grade school teachers	73
Druggists, pharmacists	72
Military officers	72
Medical doctors	67
Policemen	60
Clergy	56
Judges	53
Bankers	36
Auto mechanics	26
TV Reporters	23
Newspaper reporters	21
Business executives	20
Congressmen	20
Lawyers	18
Car Salesmen	9

■ High
■ Very High

[1] Based on data available starting 1999
Source: US Gallup Poll, November 2004

"Right now I'm between core values."

Losing Credibility

Leaders who find themselves frustrated by their inability to get people to cooperate with them on the tasks vital to the success of their companies can probably trace this failure to a lack of trust that has developed among one or more important stakeholder groups. A leader doesn't have to break promises on the level that executives at Enron and AIG did to breed mistrust. One obvious example is when a CEO promises Wall Street a certain result and fails to deliver. But a disingenuous advertising campaign is equally damaging. A corporate image program that proclaims "Employees are our most important asset" while the company is at the same time laying off great numbers of people is not going to resonate with the employees who remain behind. As a result, the next time the CEO asks for sacrifice and team effort, he is less likely to get it.

Trust is harder than ever to cultivate, primarily due to a few well-publicized examples of executives who have been lax in carrying out their responsibilities to their stakeholders. Globally, this failure of

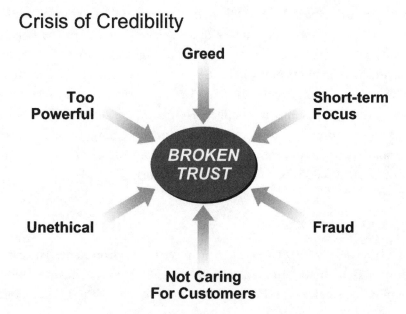

Crisis of Credibility

Greed

Too
Powerful

Short-term
Focus

BROKEN
TRUST

Unethical

Fraud

Not Caring
For Customers

trust and focus on shortsighted, greedy, or unethical behavior has greatly affected the ability of leaders to do their jobs.

Job Insecurity

As a result of these new attitudes toward corporate leaders, the premature departure of a CEO is no longer the exception; it is the rule. CEOs worldwide can now expect to spend only three years in their current positions, and 40 percent of all new CEOs will lose their jobs within eighteen months.[4] According to a recent study by the human resource consultant Drake, Beam & Morin, a CEO appointed after 1985 was three times more likely to be fired than a CEO appointed prior to that date. Only one in four companies worldwide kept the same CEO during the 1990s, half (51 percent) of all CEOs hold their position for less than three years, and 72 percent have been in office for less than five. Only 12 percent have been in their position for a decade or more.[5] And at the start of 2006, eight of the thirty companies in the Dow Jones Industrial Average began the year with a different CEO than they had twelve months earlier.[6]

The Wall Street Journal likened the year 2005 to that of 1989, comparing the symbolic, powerful imagery of the fall of the Berlin Wall to the "fall of a string of powerful chief executives."[7] Arthur Levitt, former chairman of the Securities and Exchange Commission, calls the transformation that's been occurring at the top executive level a "vast cultural change." He places the blame squarely at the top, arguing "the common catalyst for this unprecedented spurt of board action and for many of the more than 100 CEO changes last month [April 2005] is nothing less than hubris."[8]

CEO Survival

How does a CEO survive in this unsettled environment? The easy answer is by maintaining shareholder value, largely measured by a company's stock price. Booz Allen Hamilton's 2004 CEO succession report found that underperformance—not ethics, not illegality, not power struggles—is the primary reason CEOs get fired.[9]

At first glance, this seems self-evident. A CEO's reputation will always be grounded in his or her ability to deliver sound financial performance. That's why CEOs have traditionally been, first and foremost, financial managers, and why indicators like profit, competitiveness, and costs loom so large in the thinking of so many leaders. The pressure to make the numbers Wall Street expects reinforces those tendencies. The market looks favorably on companies that meet quarter-to-quarter targets and punishes those who do not. We've all seen the Street's harsh reaction when earnings deviate even slightly from forecasts and expectations. This trend has become even more pronounced as hedge funds have assumed control of a higher percentage of traded assets. It's no wonder that corporate leaders sometimes take short-term measures to temporarily boost performance, like a onetime sale of an asset, or booking a large order prematurely.

But there is a fatal flaw in this strategy. For CEOs, indeed for anyone responsible for a profit center, the most obvious way to keep their job may be to make certain the company or division meets short-term targets. The problem is that no company's stock price rises in an endless line. Every company goes through business cycles with varying levels of performance.

Fortunately for some, unfortunately for others, we have entered a new era in which financial performance is no longer the only predictor of CEO longevity. In this new environment, financials are important, but only insofar as they are a measure of leadership success. Simply getting your stock to soar or posting spectacular yearly results is no longer enough. Today's more sophisticated stakeholders consider those only partial measurements of performance. Over the long term, a leader can only survive the inevitable financial ups and downs by convincing a company's various stakeholders that he or she is the person with the drive and vision to keep the company on its best course. A mark of success is the ability to inspire trust in others.

A Matter of Values

Corporate social responsibility has become so frequently discussed that it has attained its own acronym, CSR. Yet too many leaders still believe that CSR is no more than window dressing—something nice to do, but not nearly as important as short-term results. Those are the leaders who tend to cut these programs when the economy softens or their results falter. But such inconsistency undermines trust, even among shareholders who used to look only at financial performance. Not only do stakeholders want to believe a company's leadership has a firm set of values, but there is also emerging evidence of a correlation between financial performance and measures of corporate social performance. (I discuss this further in chapter 2.)

"The real goal of corporations these days is high performance with high integrity," explains Ben Heineman, GE's senior vice president for law and public affairs during the prosperous Jack Welch years. "The critical secret sauce is how you interrelate these two elements into

"Someday we'll all look back on this and lie to a grand jury about it."

your systems and processes. And then how do you create a culture so that people are complying with both the law and with the ethical standards your company has adopted, not just because if you don't, you'll be punished, but because you want to? Ethical behavior must be internalized so that it's not something people do because they're afraid of getting caught, but because it's something they believe is right." (Ben Heineman; in discussion with the author, February 2006.)

Values and Profits

There are plenty of examples of companies that have flourished while pursuing a value-based corporate strategy. Daniel Vasella, chairman and CEO of the pharmaceutical company Novartis, believes that Novartis's strong financial results are "the consequence of good work."[10] Vasella is a strong advocate for making corporate social responsibility a part of a company's business plan. He believes his company's core value should be to "develop innovative medicines to ease suffering and cure diseases," and its corporate purpose not to develop me-too, salable products of limited market need.

Vasella has shown that eschewing a philosophy of maximizing profit no matter what does not have to yield poor financial results. In fact, putting this personal value system into practice as a corporate goal has further fueled the company's financial performance, which stands out among its competitors. "It may sound trite," says Vasella, "but I truly believe your ability to keep your shareholders' faith in the company in the end depends not on whether you 'make the quarter,' but on who you are, what your guiding principles in life are, and your behavior."[11]

A Strong Set of Values Will Disarm Your Critics

Most critics really care about the actions taken by your company. They probably have very specific objections, and because communications now go worldwide in a nanosecond, they have the ability to spread negative information rapidly to employees, customers, Wall

Street, and your other stakeholders. But they can also spread positive information just as quickly. Smart leaders don't resist or avoid
their critics. Instead, they make room at the table and engage them
in two-way communication. The goal is to open a frank dialogue—
and make warranted changes so that significant critics know you are
listening to their concerns. Once that happens they will, amazingly
enough, grow quieter. They may even begin helping you to communicate some of your positive messages. Approaching critics in the
right way begins by opening a dialogue with the most powerful people, who have the longest reach, among your most important stakeholders. Remember that your critics can come from any of the other
stakeholder groups—investors, employees, customers, or NGOs. Often they come from all these groups simultaneously. There is an in-
terconnectivity among these populations that never existed prior to
their ability to so easily communicate with each other.

   You can learn a lot by investigating what is being said about
your company in blogs. Send representatives to significant NGO
meetings and ask for personal meetings with major critics. And
when you get there, avoid defensiveness. Don't try to justify your actions; just listen for a while. Do your best to understand their objections and objectives. Sometimes you may have made assumptions
about their goals that are far from the truth. Your aim should be to
find any common ground and leverage them to achieve common
goals. But even if you can't, be sure to get the conversation to the
point (perhaps not in your first meeting) where you can agree to disagree. Then maintain communications about what you are doing to
deal with their concerns. You never know when an action you take
will change minds.

Adopting a Genuine Leadership Brand

   True leadership goes well beyond the concept—popular in my
field—of "reputation management." Most companies have entire
armies of wizards behind their curtains trying to create an image acceptable to the market. But becoming a trusted CEO is about creating

substance upon which to base an image or reputation. Even wizards can't be successful with an image that is divorced from reality. The thinking of the leaders and the reputation they seek cannot be in total disconnect. CEOs are subject to greater scrutiny than ever, so they have to be consistent from moment to moment and genuine in their external statements. An army of critics and activists is watching, so public, and private, comments must reflect the reality of your leadership and the current status of your company—or someone is going to call you on it. The values projected by Vasella at Novartis and Browne at BP, for example, are respected by their stakeholder groups because both men truly believe in the course they have set for themselves and their companies.

Great leaders create trust in the mind of stakeholders. The leaders of successful companies respond quickly and openly to challenges; they are trusted to do the right thing. These are the hardy companies, the envy of their peers, which seem to win the competitive game more often than not. And they are the companies whose leaders tend to have the longest tenures in the top job. The drivers of trust include successful financial performance, but also transparency, ethical performance, and a willingness to listen to critics. Listen at least twice as much as you speak. Yes, you've heard it all your corporate life, but how often do you really practice it? Investors, employees, customers, and critics all know something that would be profitable for you to learn. Your job is to make these bottom-up communications function well. If you aren't receiving honest, comprehensive feedback, look at your past reactions to "bad news." Perhaps you have convinced your stakeholders, especially your employees, that it's dangerous to be the bearer of negative news. Or perhaps the systems you have in place to collect information are not gathering the right information or not transmitting it to the people who can use it most effectively. Find out where these communications bottlenecks are so that you can begin to resolve them.

The particular ways in which a leader develops and uses the power of trust can create a powerful identity for both a company and its CEO. Perhaps the most important characteristic of trusted leaders

Drivers of Trust

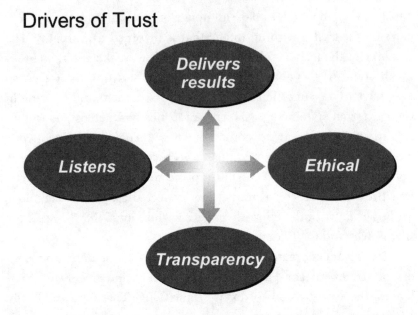

is the adoption of a leadership style that genuinely fits their personality and passion. The media tends to personalize a company's successes and failures, focusing stories around the individual who leads it. The personality of the CEO and what he stands for are essential elements in building confidence in corporate leadership. People respond to and develop opinions about individuals much more easily than about organizations. The leadership brand, therefore, takes on added importance and needs to be proactively managed.

Leadership brand is the identity each corporate leader adopts as his or her outer garment. Brand, when it comes to leaders no less than products, allows each leader to be summed up in a few words: "bold and innovative," "friendly and comforting," "ruthless and profit-minded." CEOs are routinely advised to put on the appropriate corporate face in order to build a reputation. But a leadership brand must be based on genuine leadership values. It must come from inside out, not the other way around. It can't be imposed on someone. For long-term success as a leader, it must be based on that individual's own core values.

Develop a True Leadership Brand

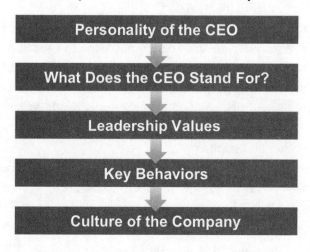

Personality of the CEO

What Does the CEO Stand For?

Leadership Values

Key Behaviors

Culture of the Company

Organizations are a web of relationships (both internal and external) that can allow leaders to move fast, change course when needed, and land on their feet when trouble hits. But those relationships will not work if there is just an empty "image" at the top. They work when your leadership conforms to the reality of what you believe. Only then can a company hope to gain, or regain, the trust of its key stakeholders.

It's not so much *what* you stand for, but that you stand for something *real*, and that you communicate that conviction openly and honestly. Even within the same industry, a leader can establish very different, but equally effective brands. Look inside yourself to create an awareness of your own attributes, and take proactive steps to create a brand that is a natural outgrowth of your own personality and expertise, your company's business mix, and the strategies you are pursuing. Defining a personal leadership brand requires intense introspection about how your personality and beliefs can be better expressed in the context of your corporation. It may help to think about what you would do if given free rein to express yourself. Don't try to mimic the leader who preceded you, even if he or she was successful and had a high profile. Jeff Immelt of GE is not going to be successful by being Jack Welch lite. He has defined his own personality in order to create his own CEO brand.

Some observers note a shift from the former charismatic CEO to the quieter, more-restrained leader. But I would argue that either personality type could succeed because genuineness is the only common denominator that inspires trust. That doesn't mean being nice to everyone. Sometimes trust can be generated by being tough on your critics, particularly if it means you are simultaneously showing support for other stakeholders.

Sometimes corporate boards purposely look for a different personality when searching for a new person to lead their company. After Hewlett-Packard's board of directors rather unceremoniously threw out one of the most visible and charismatic corporate leaders, Carly Fiorina, they turned to a lower-key leader in Mark Hurd, who did not welcome public visibility. On the other hand, Apple Computer limped along until it asked Steve Jobs, its former CEO and founder and one of the most dynamic business leaders in the United States, to return to the company. It is not personality type that dictates success or failure. It is the combination of the CEO's leadership values and the implementation of that vision across his or her portfolio of responsibilities.

Once you have developed a leadership brand that incorporates your personality and personal beliefs, your next task is to instill these leadership patterns into your organization. Cascading values and tenets of behavior into an organization is a dynamic, constant process. You can never consider that you have finished the task. By communicating your values to every stakeholder group, and by your behavior, you are continually projecting onto your organization a way of doing business.

A Web of Interlocking Bits of Information

The behaviors powerful enough to inspire trust are different for each group of stakeholders, yet they all have one thing in common: a desire to enhance connectivity. Rather than thinking of communications as a one-way process that goes from an organization to its stakeholders, think of it as a web of interlocking bits of information. Communicate outwardly through corporate messages and symbolism, as well as through your leadership brand behaviors.

Because of the revolutionary power of the Internet, these interlocking parts are in constant communications every hour of every day. To enhance trust in this new environment, you should be intensely focused on capturing messages from each stakeholder. Corporations that do an exceptional job of producing loyalty in stakeholders also facilitate communications *among* those stakeholders. That may mean anything from helping employees contribute to their communities to inspiring customers or NGOs to help gain the cooperation of regulators.

Common Characteristics

In addition to establishing a genuine leadership brand, successful leaders use a number of other critical behaviors to generate trust among their stakeholders. They are the common characteristics which I have observed to be present in leaders whose companies seem to thrive (or at least survive) no matter what the world throws at them. They flow from their constant awareness of the pitfalls that await anyone who aspires to be a leader, and they allow successful leaders to do their jobs effectively in both good times and bad. These leaders are by no means without ego, but they are able to put their ego aside when it matters. They recognize that sometimes they are going to look bad or have to make sacrifices for the good of their company. Opportunities to be second-guessed are amplified in this era of instantaneous communication and activist Wall Street analysts, but aware leaders are prepared for that. They find ways to constantly communicate the idea that success is an incremental process that takes time and effort. To them, even small movements in a positive direction, on a wide variety of measures, reflect progress to be valued and celebrated.

Since the enactment of Sarbanes-Oxley, a CEO's failure to follow a strict set of corporate governance standards will not only get him in trouble with the law, it will tarnish his reputation and undermine his position. But just following the law in today's new environment is not enough. Given the weaknesses of human behavior, personal and corporate codes of conduct must be embraced fully by corporations and their top management. Trusted leaders will make certain their efforts extend beyond the legal requirements, to instilling a strong code within the company, personally endorsing it, and showing a genuine dedication to following strict tenets of corporate behavior.

Be Honest

Successful CEOs don't hide when something goes wrong. They don't assign blame, and they don't allow mistakes to compound themselves. Instead, they respond like competent, caring human beings, the same way they would if they had no financial or political stake in the matter. They don't blunt their responses to save embarrassment to the company because they realize that the embarrassment will come, if not now, then later, after all the sordid details are dragged out, as they inevitably will be. And they don't listen to the lawyers exclusively. Taking a visible, strong position when a problem is discovered will almost always minimize its impact. A failure to apply these principles will *always* end badly.

It is not fear of discovery that motivates successful leaders to be transparent. It is, rather, a deeply ingrained sense that truthfulness will minimize, as much as possible, the consequences of bad news. Why not choose the time and manner of disclosure yourself? Admit to mistakes as soon as they occur and as fully as possible. It is never easy to dash expectations and deliver the news that weaknesses are greater than previously thought. But not telling the truth in troubled times will ultimately destroy trust in your leadership.

In an era when rumor or fact can spread globally in twenty-four hours or less, leaders had better be certain they have good relationships with and ready access to their most important stakeholders. In communicating with these groups, don't overpromise. Instead, show strong leadership by sharing all of the news, good and bad. Above all, don't lie. Don't lie to journalists, don't lie to shareholders, don't lie to employees, and don't lie to special interest groups that oppose you. A "no comment" is the appropriate response to questions you would rather not answer. And most important, don't lie to yourself.

Have Courage

It takes courage to be personally accountable and publicly take responsibility. You and your company are going to make mistakes. If blame must be assigned, the best leaders learn to accept it willingly and take steps to correct the problems underlying those complaints. Accepting blame and making changes is the only real way to get past shortcomings quickly and effectively. Unfortunately, that's not the way it works in many organizations. Those who deliver bad news are much more likely to get fired or sued (or both) than praised or even paid attention to. Such people should, instead, be your best friends. Treat these insiders as the most dedicated and loyal employees you have. After all, they are often risking everything for the good of your business, and they're showing you where improvements need to be made.

Have the courage to strike a new path by walking away from a broken business model, even if it means risking stakeholder anger. It is difficult to know when to cut losses and sharply change the course of a company. A bold move will raise skepticism among internal and external audiences, but a strong vision and clarity about values and goals can sustain the company. It can also be the motivation needed on the long road to success.

The Stakeholders

CEOs must use these trust-building behaviors to gain the trust of an ever-increasing number of stakeholders, every one of whom has become more powerful in recent years. They are emboldened by the new equalizing powers given to them by the Internet and the conviction that the unfettered operation of the free market does not always produce the best results for companies or the environment. In order to earn their trust, each of these stakeholders must be looked at individually and treated according to their unique characteristics.

Who are these stakeholders who can be inspired by the power of trust? They are:

1. Shareholders and directors
2. Employees
3. Customers
4. Policy makers
5. Nongovernmental organizations
6. The communities in which the company operates

Stakeholder Trust

1. **Shareholders and the board of directors: Inform openly to sustain confidence.** A new breed of aggressive shareholders has emerged. They feel empowered to pressure management and sometimes cross the traditional line between investors and management to try to influence company strategy and operations. They use news channels to raise the visibility of their demands. Their stories are often given top exposure, which can diminish the credibility of and confidence in corporate management. At

the same time, the board of directors, once considered an extension of the CEO, is now an independent body judging the CEO's performance. Timely information flow and discussions about strategy all need to ensure that the board and management are aligned. For example, Time Warner chairman and CEO Richard Parsons, with the support of his board, was able to resist organized and aggressive pressure from corporate raider Carl Icahn. Icahn was demanding a restructuring and asset spin-offs, as well as management changes, to boost the stock price. Evidently, Parsons and his board were in alignment.

Nothing shakes the confidence of Wall Street like surprises. Conversely, a commitment to accountability and transparency goes a long way toward retaining the trust of investors. Open and honest communication with shareholders and analysts will encourage them to give your company a fair shake. And don't underestimate the importance of keeping board members on your side by sharing both successes and problems. Straight talk must begin at the top, with the CEO or other top executives sharing both good and bad news on a timely basis. Being forthcoming only about successes can no longer be sustained in this era that demands transparency. Bad news will always find its way to the surface, and probably sooner than you think.

Sustaining confidence means appropriately managing expectations by avoiding overstating business performance. The rather obvious notion that it's extremely risky to practice financial deception in such a punishing regulatory environment is finally sinking in. Also encouraging is that more and more leaders are walking away from the tyranny of short-term performance expectations, and they are not being punished for it. The CEO of Progressive Insurance, Glenn Renwick, was one of the first to stop publishing quarterly earnings projections altogether, replacing them with monthly reports to Wall Street of actual results. "It's easier and better to run a company that way," explains Renwick. "With such transparent reporting, we aren't trying to hit anyone else's numbers."[12]

2. **Employees: Engage with continuous outreach.** At many companies facing hard times, dramatic action is needed to convince this key stakeholder group that it should do whatever it can to help management turn things around. In April 2003, when Fred Hassan was named chairman and CEO of the pharmaceutical giant Schering-Plough, he took over a company that had lost two-thirds of its market value in three years. Its most important products were approaching the end of their patents, and the pipeline for new products was dry. Hassan had to ensure the cooperation of a distrustful workforce as he transformed Schering-Plough into a leaner, future-focused company. During his first days he established that he would always tell the truth, even if the news was bad. He communicated through his actions that he needed the participation of employees at all levels of the company. He even closed the executive lunchroom to encourage top executives to mingle with other employees. At the same time that he was issuing a bleak earnings report and slashing the dividend, he outlined an internal cost-cutting plan. He sold a corporate jet and canceled most bonuses. Some employees were distressed by his actions, but most embraced them as a welcome change from the previous executive team, which had spent so much time explaining away promises it hadn't been able to keep.

For Hassan, the first rule of good people management is integrity. If you want to engender a loyal, honest, hardworking workforce, you must display those traits yourself and continually communicate them to employees. The best way to do that is to establish multiple avenues of two-way communications. Solicit e-mail from employees and read it. Work hard to listen to and address employee concerns with regular visits to where customer contacts are taking place. By showing you are interested and engaged, you can recruit employees as your business partners. If they feel they are in an ownership environment, they will respond by doing things owners do, such as coming up with useful new ideas and taking responsibility for getting the job done. Find new ways to celebrate employee successes that go beyond a certificate for the wall or a token gift. Some companies give tangible benefits, like additional time off; others simply reward employees by using their suggestions to improve the product or the work environment.

Making people feel they are listened to will go a long way toward developing employees who fight for the success of the company. At many DaimlerChrysler plants, employees are encouraged to stop the line as soon as they see a problem that may harm product quality. They also participate in lean manufacturing and product quality initiatives, which ensure that suggestions from line workers are taken seriously and worked through to a conclusion. Best of all from the employee's point of view, any profit generated contributes to employee profit sharing. Despite the company's other financial problems, this sense that the worker on the lowest rung can ferret out profit possibilities—or stop losses—has energized Chrysler plants across North America.

Remember that employees have high expectations of their leaders. Executives who think their employees will simply be grateful they have a job are likely to be disappointed. Buffeted by the volatile, globalization-driven economy, employees aren't inclined to deliver their loyalty and peak performance to just any employer. They need to be encouraged by leaders who understand that employee productivity can be a significant driver of financial performance.

3. **Customers: Listen and honestly communicate.** The notion that it's important to stay close to your customers has been around for a long time, but in too many companies it continues to be more of a slogan than a reality. Many companies still do not have systems in place to respond quickly and effectively when customers have problems with products they bought in good faith. Use technology to your advantage, but also to the advantage of your customers. Is it really good customer service to ask for an account number when it has already been entered, sometimes more than once? Automating routine transactions is fine, but systems should be put in place to ensure that employees

truly listen to the needs and expectations of customers, and then feed that critical information back to those who need to hear it.

An emphasis on efficiency and cost cutting to the detriment of actively listening to what your customers want will generally cost more than it saves. Customers want to make an emotional connection with those they do business with. They want employees to show that their business is appreciated. That doesn't mean fawning over them or showering them with gifts. It simply means keeping promises and fixing what goes wrong, and doing your best to give them what they want—not what you want to give them.

For many companies, a lack of this kind of focus is the key to understanding their shortcomings. Volkswagen AG has faced falling sales in recent years, a situation mystifying to top management, which was focused on engineering innovation. CEO Bernd Pischetsrieder, charged with reversing the trend, eventually admitted that the company's "biggest problem" was "too little customer focus." Rather than allowing customers to dictate product, he acknowledged, "VW managers and engineers paid too much attention to technology and features that customers didn't necessarily want to pay for." Pischetsrieder is restructuring Volkswagen AG to build a culture with a customer focus, particularly in the United States, where tastes differ from those in Europe. Of course, it takes time to change a deeply rooted culture. But employees are learning to interrogate each technical change to make sure it accords with customer preferences. "Sometimes in a situation like this, you just need different thinking—I don't say better or worse thinking, just different thinking—to give a signal to the internal organization that we need a different approach," says Pischetsrieder.[13]

Companies that want to retain the trust of customers also readily admit their failings. After Jayson Blair was discovered to have fabricated a number of stories that appeared in *The New York Times,* Chairman and CEO Arthur Sulzberger Jr. assigned investigative reporters to expose the newspaper's shortcomings. Sulzberger was adamant that "100 percent disclosure" was vital in order to win back the trust and confidence of *Times* readers.[14] Being forthcoming worked wonders: Readership increased after the exposure of the Blair case. But once customer service standards have been raised and promises have been made about the future, competitors and others can be counted on to hold you to them. The *Times* was taken to task for initially soft-pedaling its coverage of the paper's handling of Judith Miller's reporting about the government's fabrications concerning weapons of mass destruction, and the leaking of the name of a CIA officer. But, again, *The New York Times* was the first paper to move to correct its coverage.

4. **Policy makers: Engage in the debate.** Because of the spectacular failure of Enron and others, stricter regulations have been put in place in virtually every industry. The new Sarbanes-Oxley law is just the most pervasive of these, ensuring that corporate boards and CEOs validate financial reports and implement internal controls to prevent fraud. Both groups are now much more cognizant of the personal liability that comes with leadership. Indeed, between 2000 and 2004, fines imposed by the SEC jumped from $500 million to $3 billion a year.[15]

But it's not just the regulators' financial controls on public companies that leaders need to be concerned about. Increasingly, food companies, tobacco companies, pharmaceutical companies, and companies whose factories influence the environment are all being leaned on by policy makers. Take, for example, the war local governments have begun to wage on childhood obesity. Schools all over the country are banning junk food in vending machines. A group of "nutrition activists" has called for an extra tax on junk foods. Not all of these are truly threatening to corporations, but congressional concern over obesity could be.[16]

The food industry is reacting. Gerber, long known for its attention to nutrition, is spending considerable resources promoting better eating choices for babies, and recently commissioned the largest study ever of infant and toddler nutrition. Kraft has, for the most part, stopped marketing unhealthy snacks to children.

Often companies learn the hard way to be sensitive to social issues that affect their business. Kraft found itself in hot water over its *Oreo Cookie Counting Book*, which asked toddlers to count a diminishing pile of Oreos as they were eaten. Senator Tom Harkin of Iowa called it an example of misguided marketing that "imprints brand loyalty on unknowing preschoolers."[17] Kraft pulled the book and other offending "advergames" from its Web site.

Engaging in the debate is not the same as lobbying. Lobbying through intermediaries is like sending an e-mail expressing love for your spouse; it's much more effective in person. To maximize the effectiveness of top management, make sure you are prepared to be convincing in a short amount of time. Be certain you can clearly define your company's policy platform and your agenda, but also the agenda of your critics. Demonstrate that you consider yourself part of the solution. It's the rare bureaucrat or politician who understands how most businesses work, so use the opportunity to share industry insight and expertise. Communicate in plain, uncompromising language. We all spend so much time talking to colleagues in jargon and shorthand that after a while it starts sounding like a real language. Imagine instead that you are talking to an old friend about what you do and you'll hit the right tone and vocabulary.

Be certain to make contact with both sides of the aisle, no matter what your personal political views. The only thing that's absolutely guaranteed in politics is that those in power will not always be in power. You need to build relationships with everyone who could possibly affect your company's fortunes, both now and in the future. Politicians (and, through them, regulators) pay attention to feedback from companies about legislation that affects jobs and revenues in their districts. Even politicians whose constituents are not directly affected will pay attention to well-thought-out programs that address problems their constituents are concerned about—or could be made to care about. Policy makers will pay attention for the simple reason that few companies make a sustained and concerted effort—beyond contributions—to directly engage with them to debate issues and discuss rules that will ultimately influence their business.

Your goal is to build trust with government officials so that you'll be considered a source of information, rather than just a cheerleader for one point of view. That's the kind of leadership brand that will take you far when you want a fair shake from policymakers.

5. **Nongovernmental organizations.** The influence and financial resources of national and international advocacy groups have soared in recent years. The number of registered NGOs increased by 25 percent between 1999 and 2004, and their revenue grew by 55 percent, from $906 billion to $1.4 trillion.[18] The most successful of these NGOs have tapped into the power of the Internet to organize and spread at an unprecedented pace their pinpointed messages about corporate behavior. Their growing effectiveness is even being recognized by popular culture. The movie *The Constant Gardener* (2005), based on a John Le Carré novel, depicted ordinary people successfully battling to stop a pharmaceutical company from killing people in Africa while testing a new drug to prevent tuberculosis. Its message was that people are empowered to challenge the actions of companies they come in contact with in their daily lives and that companies are more than ever vulnerable to the actions of outsiders. That's exactly the sentiment that has made NGOs such a powerful force in the lives of many corporations.

6. **Community: Commit to corporate social responsibility.** The days are long past when a company could operate in isolation, not considering either its local communities or its footprint around the globe. Communities, in turn, are increasingly scrutinizing the actions of their corporate citizens. While tax breaks continue to be used to attract corporate investment, more and more communities are asking whether certain companies are worthy additions to their municipal space. The most prominent

current example is Wal-Mart, which has famously been chased away from some communities, including Chicago and many areas of California. Despite efforts, the retailer failed to completely establish its credibility as a caring and fair employer. Outsiders—that is, community leaders—have been able to sell their own story of a selfish behemoth only interested in profiting at the expense of employees and community retailers.

Becoming involved in the communities where you operate is not just about throwing money at a problem. Good works are much more likely to deteriorate into mere gestures if you are not certain that you are applying the right solutions on the ground, solutions that people want. That means treating these programs as a business function like any profit center. It's just that results are measured by the ability to create a groundswell of trust. Community members will be the first to question your integrity if they sense corporate-sponsored programs are simply intended to make a company look good.

Companies have also learned not to pursue a problem unless they bring some part of the solution to the table.[19] Be prepared to partner with another company or institution with the expertise to accomplish a specific, ambitious task. If you run an oil company, you probably don't have the expertise to combat hunger on your own. But you might use your logistics expertise to partner with a transportation company or a food distributor to make sure shipments arrive when and where they are needed. Partnering with an NGO can also provide the endorsements that make it easier to cut through local red tape.

Remember also the old adage that "no good deed goes unpunished." Critics will always be looking for the black lining in any silver cloud. Think about the factors in your community programs that might provide fodder for criticism, and either make changes or prepare yourself to respond forcefully and accurately. You don't want criticism to damage a legitimate program. Even misguided criticism can undermine your credibility and any trust you hope to create.

Advance the Agenda

Most people want to live lives that are meaningful, and leaders of successful corporations have more opportunity than most to do that. Leaders who tap into core beliefs and communicate their commitment to them earn the trust of their key stakeholders. They use the power of trust to help motivate each stakeholder group to support actions that will prove to be of long-term benefit to their company. They advance the agenda by changing behaviors before pressures from third parties or policy makers impose the changes from outside. If you set the agenda, you operate from a position of strength and avoid having someone else tell your story.

Successful leaders stay focused on what is important to long-term success, rather than being stampeded into actions they may later regret. They can be identified fairly easily by the values that they and their employees project to the world. They are inspired by an adherence to principles that form, for each of them, a platform of rock-solid values that they will not violate. Know them by the trust they engender across stakeholder groups, the admiration they garner in the marketplace, their performance in the long term, and often by their ability to retain their position until they choose to leave.

2

Profitable Responsibility

You must be the change you wish to see in the world.

Mahatma Gandhi[1]

When competent people are inspired by the purpose of their work they can achieve extraordinary things.

Daniel Vasella, M.D.,
Chairman and CEO, Novartis
(in discussion with author)

ACCORDING TO A July-August 2005 Roper poll,[2] only 2 percent of Americans believe that CEOs of large companies are "very trustworthy." Two percent! That's a serious problem for CEOs and their companies. Anything that dilutes the enthusiasm of consumers and investors will ultimately have an impact on their willingness to purchase both products and shares of stock.

The loss of credibility with consumers and other key stakeholders has of course been influenced by Enron- and WorldCom-like corporate scandals. But it's also been exacerbated by a steady stream of news about layoffs, job outsourcing to the developing world, dismantling of pension plans, and sky-high executive salaries.

One sector that has been particularly hard hit by trust and

credibility issues is the pharmaceutical industry. A January 2005 Wall Street Journal/NBC News poll found that only 3 percent of people surveyed thought that drug companies were working for the public good. Seventy-six percent thought they were mostly interested in making a profit.[3] Pharmaceutical companies also rank poorly in the annual Reputation Quotient study, developed by the Louis Harris organization and the Reputation Institute in New York.[4] The exception is Johnson & Johnson, which actually derives a lot of revenues from pharmaceuticals and medical devices, but retains the perception of being a baby products company.

Pharmaceutical companies are in a unique position because of the love-hate relationship consumers have with them. On the one hand, the medicines they manufacture save the lives of millions of Americans each year. On the other hand, many people resent high drug prices and the industry's double-digit profit margins. Their reputation was further damaged by the controversy over their responsibility to provide medicines to impoverished patients in need, particularly in Africa. After large demonstrations were held in South Africa and elsewhere demanding access to AIDS medications, events reached a crisis in late 1997 when South Africa passed legislation allowing small local companies to produce their own version of drugs on which another pharmaceutical company held the patent. The law also allowed the government to import AIDS drugs from countries that didn't respect international patent law. The major pharmaceutical companies immediately filed suit against the South African government for patent violations. The lawsuit became tied up in South Africa's Constitutional Court, creating hostility on all sides.

In recent years, however, the acrimonious debate has largely subsided. This is the result of a decision on the part of governments, industry, and nongovernmental organizations to cooperate in an effort to help patients gain access to the medicines they need. Pharmaceutical companies are currently donating tens of millions of dollars' worth of AIDS medicines to patients in third world countries, and contribute millions more to the complex job of creating the infrastructure and resources necessary for diagnosis and distribution.

A recent International Pharmaceutical Industry Association survey showed that during the five years from 2000 to 2005, the industry contributed about $4.4 billion and donated more than 540 million treatments to the developing world.[5]

Over the years, some pharmaceutical companies have contributed reluctantly, or not at all, to humanitarian efforts, while others understood early on why such efforts to go "beyond profits" should become part of their daily business practices. Those that have shown compassion for patients in need and a strong commitment to keeping the patient at the center of their efforts are clearly the better for it. During his ten years as CEO of the pharmaceutical giant Novartis, Daniel Vasella has demonstrated that it is indeed possible to combine personal values, corporate social responsibility, and ethics with profit and growth. By Vasella's own admission, "The pharmaceutical industry has a bad image in part because of our own behavior. Price increases, aggressively protecting patents when the patent life has expired, and access to medicines in developing countries, principally related to AIDS, I think these were three areas where we should have been better inspired."[6] But Vasella is committed to changing that reputation during his tenure at Novartis.

The Case for Values

A number of factors have combined to make ethics and responsibility vital ingredients of a sound corporate strategy. Companies today interact with a far broader range of stakeholders than ever before, including investors, employees, communities, governments, and NGOs. With so many interested parties, carrying out commercial operations in an ethical manner and proactively assuming responsibilities in society that extend beyond bottom-line results builds trust for a company and for its management across a broad swath of society. And just as greater trust leads directly to more effective employee retention, higher sales, and more repeat business, actions which create a reason to question that trust are, in contrast, likely to have swift and potentially catastrophic results.

Another reason ethics and responsibility have become integral to the workings of successful companies is that corporate actions can no longer be conducted under the radar. The number of media channels has exploded, the speed of news has accelerated, and the reach of information is now global. As a result, corporate managers are increasingly in the spotlight. Their behavior must be assumed to be constantly on display and under scrutiny. This does not have to be a negative development, however. In this media-saturated age, a business's visible engagement in the communities in which it operates is much more likely to penetrate the consciousness of people who in previous years might have paid it little attention. Corporate responsibility, therefore, is fundamental to a company's reputation.

Executives who look up from the short-term numbers in order to integrate ethics and responsibility into their decisions will likely enjoy long-term benefits. For one thing, the more the image of an industry or a company suffers in the media, the more likely it will become a target for politicians, regulators, and voters demanding changes in behavior and in leadership. Customers, too, will either be attracted or repelled by a company's ethical behavior. Legal guilt or innocence is sometimes besides the point. Despite the fact that the accounting firm Arthur Andersen had a guilty verdict overturned by an appeals court in the Enron case, it was a pyrrhic victory. By the time Andersen received the favorable court ruling, it was already bankrupt. Loss of trust in Andersen made clients flee as soon as major trouble started brewing.

The power of trust has also been magnified as corporations have taken on the personality of their leaders. CEOs becoming "the face" of their companies have made the public feel more connected to public corporations. This has a powerful impact in both good times and bad. Ken Lay and Jeff Skilling became Enron, and Dennis Koslowski became Tyco. On the flip side, however, personalities also have the potential to humanize business and build trust. Goldman Sachs international vice chairman Bob Hormats calls this dichotomy the "values gap," and believes that the United States in particular has

"Miss Dugan, will you send someone in here who can distinguish right from wrong?"

had a bad case of it. "If a CEO has values, he's an example, and if he doesn't, that's an example, too," says Hormats. "I think good values are essential qualities and have to be front and center."[7]

Hormats points out that we have recently experienced an "ethics deficit," with the reemergence of a culture in which, "when it comes to making money, anything goes." He warns, "Breaches in ethics, accountability, and trust can do enormous damage. Business and financial leaders of the twenty-first century will be judged not simply on their ability to build or manage strong companies and make money, but also on the virtues they practice in their professional and personal lives."[8]

Employees want to work for companies that are well respected for their ethical standards. The best employees are likely to seek values that inspire them to do great things for the company, for themselves, and for their community. Nothing makes people work harder than believing that their place of employment is doing good for the world. Steven Perlstein, a reporter for *The Washington Post*, observed a few years ago that "whenever the subject of community involvement comes up in conversations with business executives, the tone of the conversation almost invariably changes. Instead of the

usual reticence, cool rationality, and measured tones, they literally
light up, talking with passion, determination, and candor."[9]

Sound values have moved to center stage as a fundamental
building block for successful management. Successful leaders can
no longer ignore the fact that a new generation of employees is coming on board, many of whom expect their employers to live up to
certain standards of behavior and make a positive contribution to
the global community. A 2003 study of undergraduates in twenty of
the world's largest economies found that "three in five undergraduates would choose to work for a company that could demonstrate its
ethical values and positive impact on society."[10] And in a survey of
the 2004 graduating class of the European business school, IMD,
more than half mentioned credibility, integrity, empathy, balance, or
helping the less advantaged when asked what they would like to be
known for. Only 10 percent agreed with the statement that the mandate of companies is to serve shareholders alone or primarily.[11]

There has been a shift in recruiting patterns, too. To recruit and
retain the best employees, companies are going to have to do more
than pay lip service to ethics and corporate citizenship at all levels of
the organization. In the 2005 *Wall Street Journal*/Harris Interactive
business school survey, 84 percent of corporate recruiters stated that
MBAs needed to demonstrate awareness and knowledge of corporate social responsibility (CSR), listing this as part of their evaluation parameters.[12] As ethics and responsibility drive trust, they also
shape it and create a resiliency that allows a company's leaders to
successfully ride the ups and downs of day-to-day, quarter-to-quarter
business fortunes. The trust that stems from a commitment to sound
values is critical to the ability of companies to do business, and for
management to sustain their positions.

Values and Performance as Equal Partners

Few CEOs or top managers would disagree that their principal responsibility is to run a financially successful company. No company
would survive for long if its business was not sound. Managers are

trained to enhance their skills so that they make good investments, beat the competition, and strive to continuously innovate. That is the stuff of good management.

Some executives believe that this means limiting charitable activities. Peter Brabeck-Letmanthe, chairman and CEO of Nestlé SA, stated in a recent speech that companies shouldn't feel obligated to "give back" to the community because they haven't taken anything away. "I think there is good reason for corporate philanthropy," he says. "But as managers, we need to be very careful, because it is not our money we're handing out, but the money of our shareholders."[13]

Businesses do actually have a legal obligation to fulfill their duties to shareholders first. This became settled case law in the United States in 1916 after Henry Ford decided to finance price cuts by canceling a quarterly dividend that the Dodge brothers, Ford stockholders, were going to use to finance a competing car company. They sued Ford, arguing that profits were the property of shareholders and could not be given to anyone else, for whatever reason. The U.S. Supreme Court agreed.[14]

Economist Milton Friedman famously argued thirty-five years ago that the business of business is business only, and that a corporation has no further obligations as long as it obeys the law.[15] This kind of sentiment would have us believe that business leaders are actually acting illegally—or at least immorally—if they don't follow this principle to the exclusion of all others. But the world has changed. Today such Scrooge-like behavior is no longer acceptable or desirable, and is not part of a successful company's corporate strategy. Certainly no court or savvy investor would argue that ethics and social responsibility are not necessary parts of winning corporate leadership. The recent spate of corporate scandals has reinforced this reality. While Wall Street and corporate boards continue to pressure management to focus on making short-term numbers, recent events have put longer-term considerations on the table. Focusing only on the short term may be the temporary answer for corporate leaders struggling to keep Wall Street happy, but it can be risky to the long-term health of their careers. We live in an era when ethical lapses are fodder for front-page headlines, often with a personal focus, and regulators are aggressively enforcement-oriented. Not only are sound values necessary to avoid an Enron-style catastrophe, but, over the long term, companies that push ethical behavior through the entire organization have found bottom-line benefits. Forward-looking CEOs are beginning to understand at a profound level that there are more important things in the lives of their companies—and careers—than simply making the numbers quarter to quarter. Successful, well-respected leaders realize that being a good corporate citizen is fundamental to a company's "license" to operate in society.

Research has confirmed the correlation between good corporate citizenship and performance. For companies to thrive over the long term in the twenty-first century, performance and values must go hand in hand. Joshua Margolis of Harvard and J. P. Walsh of the University of Michigan recently analyzed ninety-five empirical studies on corporate social performance and financial performance. They found that about nine times as many studies revealed a positive correlation between social and financial performance as those that indicated a negative one.[16] Another indication of the long-term earnings potential for companies with a values focus is the Dow Jones Sustainability Index (DJSI) and the FTSE4Good Indices. Both track a portfolio of the top 10 percent of U.S. companies most committed to long-term economic, environmental, and social strategies. These companies focus on innovation and sound governance and are concerned with stakeholder interests and steady financial growth through productivity gains, competitiveness, and reputation. The DJSI defines corporate sustainability as a business approach that creates long-term shareholder value by embracing opportunities and managing risks derived from economic, environmental, and social developments. These companies integrate long-term economic, environmental, and social aspects in their business strategies while maintaining global competitiveness and brand reputation. They foster loyalty by investing in customer-relationship management and product and service innovation, and they set the highest standards of corporate governance and stakeholder engagement, including corporate codes of conduct and public reporting. And they manage human resources in a way that satisfies employees.

Since its launch in 1999, the DJSI has outperformed the major world stock markets,[17] and the FTSE4Good Index has either closely tracked or outperformed the FTSE All-Share Index.[18] The FTSE, best known for the FTSE 100, an index of blue-chip stocks on the London Stock Exchange, is similar to Standard & Poor's in the United States.[19]

Doing Good Means Doing Well at Novartis

Just as one needs a strategic plan to ensure profitable growth, leaders must also have a plan in order to focus on sustaining trust with key stakeholders. When Daniel Vasella became CEO of Novartis in 1996 following the merger of Ciba-Geigy and Sandoz, he wanted to shake up the old-line Swiss drug company. He realized that it would take time to build a new culture, but his early efforts started the process of creating a company with a clear purpose and a culture built on performance and strong values. Vasella, along with his management team, formulated a clear statement of the company's purpose: "We want to discover, develop, and successfully market innovative products to cure diseases, to ease suffering, and to enhance the quality of life."[20]

He also made certain that all executives knew what they were responsible and accountable for, and he insisted on a regular and thorough performance evaluation process. He put in place a pay-for-performance system that reached deep into the company's ranks and democratized communications so that all associates were informed about company goals, strategy, and results. "While performance in our core businesses remains our primary responsibility and contribution to society, doing the right thing in the right way will preserve the license to operate and make our business sustainable," says Vasella. Vasella believed that in order to achieve a strong commitment to corporate governance, he would need to put in place a values-based management process that was clear to everyone who worked at Novartis. The process included a plan with goals, strategy, regulations, and standards that Vasella publicly endorsed so that the commitment at the top was evident.

Cascading Ethics and Responsibility into an Organization

"We had a unique opportunity to start with a new company and build a new culture," recalls Vasella, referring to how he, along with his management team, integrated Sandoz and Ciba-Geigy to become Novartis. "Top management, with the support of the board of directors, felt it important to set a defined purpose, aspirations, and values which would guide our common behavior." Vasella says it was also important to communicate throughout the new company not only the change in philosophy, but also the new management structure.

According to Joerg Reinhardt, CEO of Novartis Vaccines and Diagnostics, using in-person meetings at every major corporate location and clear, timely information, "from day 15 or 20 after the merger, everyone understood what the new culture was going to be and who was in charge of what." Indeed, at every opportunity Vasella proclaimed to his management that "the mix of trust and integrity [is] key" to the company's success and that he hoped everyone would "have an understanding of where the journey goes." He also took some creative steps to illustrate the values of leadership. In 1999, for example, at the company's annual management meeting in Interlaken, Switzerland, Vasella invited former Israeli prime minister Shimon Peres to be the keynote speaker. "This man is a statesman; he has wisdom," Vasella told his managers when introducing Peres. "His pain, hard work, persistence, and vision and hopes are clear. We believe that *our* vision will keep us going as a company." (Daniel Vasella remarks at the Novartis Management Meeting, January 2001.)

At the management meeting in 2001, Vasella again emphasized the importance of aligning the company around values. He pointed out that the organization was like a Rothko painting in the way its associates come together to "adapt to the background, the market environment . . . with an alignment with each other in terms of direction." Again he stressed the importance of creating a climate of "mutual trust and support."[21] He talked about corporate social responsibility being a "line responsibility, part of the daily business." It was then a matter of implementation, attracting the right people and creating the right incentives for building a high-performance organization focused on innovation. "Of course," he concluded, "it requires years of consistent work to build a common culture in a large, global company, which encompasses associates with various backgrounds. While fundamentals are constant, the new environment in which we work sets new challenges, so we have to continuously learn and adapt."

The message clearly had an impact. An independent survey of Vasella's management team in 2001 showed that 78 percent agreed that they shared a set of clear values and a clear corporate purpose.[22] In an effort to illustrate to employees that the company's values were in line with successful commercial objectives, Vasella completely revamped the design and content of the annual report, using the theme "Caring and Curing." Photos portraying the suffering, but also the benefits of medicine, as well as patient profiles from the developing world, reinforced the company's purpose to stakeholders. A corporate advertising campaign—with the tagline "Think what's possible"—also focused on patient case histories to give external audiences, as well as employees, a sense of the determination across the company that their work impact the lives of patients and their families. Adhering to the company's values and vision, Vasella believes, "allows people and organizations to achieve more than they ever dreamed they could. Ordinary people become extraordinary people, achieving together extraordinary things."

Novartis's intranet site is used to make certain everyone working at Novartis has a clear understanding of acceptable and unacceptable behavior. Case studies of instances when employees, including management, disregarded Novartis's internal rules are posted for everyone at Novartis to see. This kind of transparency is aimed at allowing every employee to understand what constitutes a violation of the company's code of conduct, and encourages appropriate measures to be taken when warranted, including additional training to decrease the incidence of misconduct. Training is crucial because, as Vasella says, "Our weakest performer determines our reputation."

Other tools used by Novartis to ensure that the intended values and ethics cascade throughout the organization include:

1. Community Partnership Day, begun in 1997 shortly after Vasella became CEO. Once a year Novartis employees are encouraged to take time off from work to give back to their community. The company provides organized groups from Novartis with transportation to and from the activity.
2. No-exceptions ethics training. Every Novartis employee is expected to complete a mandatory online training course on ethical behavior.
3. Zero tolerance on ethics violations. Employees are constantly made aware of the company's zero tolerance policy in regard to ethical violations.

Harvard University's John Quelch and V. Kasturi Rangan support Vasella's thesis that good citizenship and healthy profits are not mutually exclusive by suggesting that companies can become more socially responsible through a process they call "strategic philanthropy." They agree that a company doesn't have to be altruistic to the exclusion of direct business benefits, and that the proper course is to leverage a company's strengths and build on them. "Identify a single initiative or class of initiatives that fits with your company's strategy, image, and capabilities," they advise.[23]

Instilling a Corporate Credo

How does a large organization guide the behavior of fifty thousand employees or more, most of whom will never meet top management and who will never even visit the company's worldwide corporate headquarters? Is the CEO in New York or Paris really responsible for the actions of a midlevel employee in Uganda or Singapore? Actually, yes.

Large corporations are like nation-states. While a CEO cannot, of course, be aware of the activities of every employee and their consequences, it is the CEO's responsibility to instill certain values and create a mandate that a violation of these values will not be tolerated. The most straightforward way to do this is through the publication and dissemination of a corporate credo, code of ethics, or mission statement. Such a statement should begin with a brief discussion of the company's purpose—its right to existence, if you will—and serve to instill a set of values and expectations. Large global companies with thousands of employees and operations in virtually every country in the world must align themselves around a single mission for their business and a set of values that dictates their behavior. In order to ensure that companies bring value to their stakeholders, those who work for the company must adhere to a moral "compact" about the way they will conduct their affairs. It need not be obfuscated by a cumbersome set of verbiage. Google's corporate code of conduct is simply "Don't Be Evil," and the company recently ranked third in the annual Reputation Quotient ranking, after Johnson & Johnson and Coca-Cola. That doesn't mean it will never be criticized, just as exhibiting trust-building behaviors will not make leaders immune to criticism. Google has been under fire recently for agreeing to censor certain Web sites in China in return for support from the Chinese government in the wide distribution of its search engine.

Simply having a credo or mission statement is not enough, of course. Codes of conduct have been made and ignored for generations. Trusted leaders, however, are able to get employees at all levels to take them seriously. For a code of conduct to have any real meaning, it must be disseminated, emphasized, and, most of all, taken to heart by senior management. After all, Enron's statement of philosophy, printed in its 2001 annual report, emphasized "communication," "respect," "integrity," and "excellence." This did nothing to stop top management from cavalierly ignoring the code of ethics or from preventing deceit at the most senior levels of that company. In fact, evaluation of what went wrong at Enron uncovered a brazenly frank culture of pushing limits. On the desk of CFO Andrew Fastow, a cube defined "communication" as "when Enron says it will rip your face off, it means it will rip your face off."[24] This willingness to do anything to achieve business goals pervaded the organization and ultimately led to its downfall.

The CEO is accountable for the conduct of the organization, and therefore must be identified with its vision and values. "Ethics has to become part of the genetic code of a company, which requires employee education and consistent behavior across the entire organization," says Daniel Vasella.[25] "Employees must understand their responsibilities and respect the boundaries expressed through laws, regulations, and the internal code of conduct, all reflecting the inherent and explicit expectations of society."

Novartis's code of conduct, instituted in 1999 and revised in 2001 to comply with the United Nations Global Compact, includes standards that must be met by all Novartis employees as they go about handling themselves ethically and safely in diverse and challenging situations. It is a comprehensive, instructive document that covers such areas as discrimination, conflicts of interest, bribes and kickbacks, insider trading, antitrust issues, compliance with the law, personal obligations, and protection of business assets.[26] Novartis takes its enforcement seriously. It has forty-five compliance officers worldwide, publishes an annual compliance report, and has a compliance Web site and training module. In 2005 the company launched an e-learning program in which employees are given explicit guidelines on bribery, gifts, insider trading, and the use of confidential information. Given that acceptable business practices vary in different parts of the world, Novartis urges associates to remember that "just because competitors, customers or distributors engage in a certain conduct," that does not mean the conduct is acceptable to Novartis.

Novartis was also among the first large companies to sign the United Nations Global Compact, an agreement to comply with nine progressive principles concerning human rights, labor, and the environment. The company then prepared an extensive audit of its operations around the world to make certain each one was compliant with everything in the code. Currently, 2,062 companies and organizations are members of the Global Compact, representing eighty countries.

Ethics in Action: The Value of Looking Outward

Stellar leaders understand that bringing values to bear on a company's day-to-day operations allows employees to feel inspired by what they do for a living. They also know that going beyond do-good rhetoric is good business. People who trust a company are more likely to choose its products than those of a company they don't know or which they feel uneasy about. According to the Natural Marketing Institute, about 30 percent of American consumers consider factors other than price and quality when buying products.[27] The most successful executives today have a new attitude toward their relationships with society. They realize the need to go beyond window-dressing efforts toward the adoption of a new social contract. According to Ian Davis, worldwide managing director of McKinsey and Company, "Shareholder value should continue to be seen as the critical measure of business success. However, it may be more accurate, more motivating—indeed more beneficial to shareholder value over the long term—to describe business's ultimate purpose as the efficient provision of goods and services that society wants. This is a hugely valuable, even noble purpose."[28]

A new type of corporate citizenship is being ingrained into the DNA of successful companies. Making this type of corporate responsibility—the kind so inspiring to Novartis employees—work will always begin at the top. "In order for a company to place a true emphasis on corporate social responsibility, its leaders have to care about other people," explains Vasella. "I have spent time in India visiting leprosy patients and in Vietnam seeing children suffering with infections that fester due to lack of antibiotics and dying from malaria and cancer. As a physician, I should be used to these afflictions and understand patients, but it is almost impossible to *really* know how it would be to grow up poor and sick in a developing country. Without external help, poverty and illness mean misery and, all too often, death."[29]

While many executives might view Vasella's compassion for the world's poor and sick as noble, but a potential drain on his bottom line, Vasella believes just the opposite. Vasella sees the company's financial performance and its duty to the world as being seamless parts of the same goal. "At Novartis, corporate citizenship means sustainable commitments to patients around the world and to our own people; to their health, safety, and the environment; to proper business conduct; and to sound corporate governance," says Vasella. "We have tangible programs in each of these areas, and we are constantly striving to improve our own performance in them. In the end, doing right makes business sense." (Daniel Vasella, in discussion with the author.)

Under Vasella, Novartis has made a commitment that the company's values are more than just words on paper. This is easy to say, but is more difficult to do when the strategy might adversely affect the company's short-term bottom line. According to Vasella, "Compassion for the suffering of others, while at the same time maintaining awareness of our own potential and latitude to help, are the foundation of any social responsibility engagement." He emphasizes that strong financial performance is necessary in order to become involved in socially responsibility activities, pointing out that "profits are like the air we breathe. We don't live to breathe, but without air we cease to live. Healthy profits are a prerequisite to even consider engaging in needed, but often costly projects that have no direct, visible return to a company or its investors."[30]

Gleevec Puts Novartis to the Test

Vasella's words were put to the test in April 1999 when unusual results began coming in related to the leukemia drug Gleevec. "I had trouble believing the data," Vasella now says, "but the numbers told the story."

All thirty-one patients who suffered from chronic myeloid leukemia (CML) in the Phase 1 trial of Gleevec experienced reductions to normal levels in their previously elevated white blood cell counts. Ordinarily a drug company would wait for further data before committing production capacity and resources, but Vasella broke with that usual practice and directed the company to move swiftly. "With such spectacular results in hand, the next steps were obvious: commit large amounts of capital and human resources to the drug. Rush the drug to market. How could we act otherwise? The lives of patients were at stake. What we really cared about were all the patients who were waiting for a better, safer, more effective drug, and Gleevec was a potentially lifesaving medicine."[31]

Cynics can be forgiven if they suspect that Vasella was more focused on the profit potential of what appeared to be an astonishingly effective drug, rather than on patient health. But the accelerated development of the product was risky. At the time, the potential patient population was considered to be less than 7,000. Vasella was forging ahead with developing Gleevec with the possibility that in the end the drug might not make it to the market at all, or never be a profitable product because of high R&D and production investments and small patient numbers. But he believed that "focusing on satisfying the needs of patients is Novartis's right of existence."[32]

Vasella continued to be an outspoken and visible cheerleader at every step in Gleevec's development process. This message from the top provided a catalyst which helped the entire management team move together quickly to meet a difficult goal. Vasella instilled confidence among internal and external stakeholders that the company was doing everything possible to quickly and responsibly make Gleevec available to all those who needed it. He even developed a personal letter-writing relationship with several patients.

After Vasella saw the early clinical results on Gleevec, he gave the development team just two years to bring the drug to market, an extremely aggressive timetable that most employees were skeptical about meeting. But in line with their chief's directive, employees delivered. Investments were made in manufacturing to expedite the

clinical development, allowing more patients to enter clinical studies and have access to Gleevec. Vasella personally made sure employees understood the importance of doing everything they could
to get the drug to market as quickly as possible. While Vasella led the
charge from the top, speeding Gleevec through the approval process
took the focused efforts of hundreds of Novartis employees, from development to manufacturing, who worked long hours, over weekends and holidays, to accelerate the pace in bringing this lifesaving
drug to market.

Vasella says he has learned—and tries hard to remember always—
that in the end it is not money that motivates people to get up every
day and go to work or increase shareholder value, but rather their
desire to feel they are making a valuable contribution. "Nobody
works to make rich people richer," he says. "With Gleevec, we saw
that employees became personally involved in the success of the
drug. Employees at the Ringaskiddy, Ireland, facility where Gleevec
was initially produced were in contact via the Internet with members of Gleevec support groups. That gave them personal connec-
tions to patients and further strengthened their commitment to get
the drug to those who needed it as quickly as possible. Employees
pressed their bosses to find ways to speed up production of the drug,
coming up with ideas and possibilities for using the equipment more
efficiently and more quickly."

Another factor that made the management of Gleevec's development and launch so effective was the willingness of Novartis's leaders to reveal their own doubts and to communicate openly. That led
to a bond of trust with key stakeholders, particularly patients and
employees.

Shortly after Gleevec was approved for treating CML, Vasella
shared with the Gleevec team a handwritten letter he had received
from a CML patient in New York. "He told me the story of his life,
sharing joys like his first Christmas with his grandson, as well as
hardships, the toughest being his diagnosis with CML in January
2001," Vasella recalls. "It was, of course, a devastating diagnosis, and
he went through many difficult treatments which he had trouble tol-

erating and which did not help curb the disease. Then his doctor told him about Gleevec, which was not yet approved. He talked about how he hoped he could hold on until the medicine was available, and that within two weeks of Gleevec's FDA approval he took his first capsule. He wrote:

> I've been taking Gleevec now for a year and a half and have been in remission for the last 8 months. I never knew who to thank for my recovery, but I would like to extend my deepest thanks to all of the people who helped the cause of this lifesaving drug.[33]

"As a physician I treated patients for many years," says Vasella. "Still, it is the greatest mark of success for me to hear the stories of patients that we at Novartis have been able to help."

To be certain that no patient would be denied access to Gleevec, Vasella put in place an international patient-assistance program. Considering the problems of diagnosis and delivery of health care in many parts of the world, there was considerable uncertainty that a global commitment of this kind could be carried out in time for the international launch. Yet the Patient Assistance Program in the United States and the Gleevec International Patient Assistance Program internationally became perhaps the most generous and far-reaching patient assistance programs ever developed on a global scale. As of 2005, three years after its implementation, Novartis had provided Gleevec free to about 15,000 patients in more than eighty countries who would not otherwise have had access to it.

Gleevec has become a model at Novartis for decreasing development time and increasing speed to market. "It also served as a reaffirmation of our purpose as a company and the values we set out to instill in the Novartis culture,"[34] says Vasella. "Some will criticize corporate citizenship efforts, commenting that they only aim to improve image. I would say that reputation is important, and in many cases it may indeed be the key driving factor behind the commitment to corporate social responsibility. But this is legitimate, as long as it leads to improved behavior."[35]

For Novartis, the results are clear. The company's revenues have consistently outpaced the industry, gaining market share quarter after quarter. In 2005 Novartis made *Fortune* magazine's World's Most Admired Companies list for the first time. During a period when market values for most of the largest pharmaceutical companies have experienced double-digit declines, Novartis's shares had double-digit increases, rising more than 16 percent in 2005.

Helping the World as a Sound Financial Strategy

Novartis is by no means alone in practicing what it preaches, while at the same time boosting financial performance. For Novartis, it was providing access to medicines with a keen sensitivity to patient needs, particularly for those in the developing world. For other companies—IBM, for example—it is giving computer technology to teachers in third world countries. Both companies are helping the world while extending the reach of their products and embracing this millennium's strategy of differentiating themselves from the competition.

AMD (formerly Advanced Micro Devices) is another company putting its pocketbook where its heart is. AMD believes it can become the number-one computer chip supplier in the developing world by investing in getting the world's poor connected to the Internet. CEO Hector Ruiz launched what he calls the 50×15 Initiative to give 50 percent of the world's population access to the Internet by 2015. He has already made giant strides in India, where AMD sells its wireless personal internet communicator (PIC) for $230, with a monthly charge of less than $10 for internet access. The sturdy little device includes a stripped-down version of Microsoft's browser, along with e-mail, word processing, and spreadsheet programs. Solectron builds the hardware, with about $30 worth of AMD parts.[36]

Ruiz likes to ask the rhetorical question, "Have you ever made a difference in your life?"[37] He is an extreme example of a CEO who wears his values on his sleeve, but who is also concerned with shareholder value. Will the PIC catch on among India's mostly poor population of one billion people, who were never before even considered a market by any other chip maker? Even Ruiz cannot say, but AMD's strategy is indicative of the viability of a new corporate contract that in today's environment Ruiz can consider without widespread criticism from his investors. Ruiz, who grew up in poverty, considers that just getting to market with the PIC is a triumph of values.

Citigroup Raises the Bar on Corporate Ethics

Even companies not previously associated with an emphasis on ethical behavior are now seeing the light. Chuck Prince, CEO of Citigroup, was not known as someone who spent much time talking about values, ethics, or shared responsibilities. He has, in fact, been described as someone who worked with Sanford Weill to "build Citigroup with a ruthless focus on cost-cutting, deal making and financial performance."[38] Yet in recent years he has committed himself to leading a sweeping ethics initiative throughout Citigroup and has famously pledged to devote half his time to the effort.

Remarkably, Prince has begun to wonder whether half his time will be enough to change attitudes at the massive Citigroup. The catalyst for Prince's decision to commit to a total focus on ethics was evidence that suggested that Citigroup had financed several companies, including Enron, WorldCom, and Parmalat, whose failures and financial wrongdoing dominated the business news for months. Citibank itself was caught up in the wave of corporate scandals when alleged inappropriate deals in Japan by its private banking arm came to light. Among other transgressions, the Citigroup units were accused of helping customers hide losses, manipulating stock prices, and misrepresenting their profits, and themselves had failed to do criminal background checks on customers, all in the service of meeting ever higher revenue goals set by headquarters.[39] At the time, Prince declared that he didn't believe the company was broken in terms of ethics, but admitted that "we emphasized the short-term performance side of the equation exclusively. We didn't think we had to say, 'And, by the way, don't violate the law.'"[40]

In October 2004 Citigroup signaled to the world a change in attitude when Prince and other Citigroup executives were photographed in Japan bowing deeply in the traditional Japanese apology stance. Ethical retraining of employees is now a top priority for Prince as he moves his initiative, known internally as the Five-Point Plan, forward.

"The Five-Point Plan developed from a series of discussions I had with employees around the world about the company we want to be and what it means to work at Citigroup," explained Prince to ethics consultant Alex Brigham. "Those discussions, along with some ethical issues we faced in some of our businesses last year, helped us realize that we needed to create more balance in our culture between achieving short-term results and maintaining a longer-term perspective on our franchise—for the sake of our clients and investors, but also for our employees."[41]

The five points Prince speaks of improving are training, talent and development, performance appraisals, communications, and controls. Senior managers—approximately three thousand employees—participate in a "Franchise Forum" which uses a case-study format to encourage discussion of the interaction of ethical responsibilities and financial results. Employees at all levels are urged to use an "ethics hotline" to report unethical behavior, and calls to that line have steadily increased. "This is not evidence," says Prince, "of increased unethical behavior. It's a sign that we are changing our culture."[42]

Institutional safeguards are being implemented to ensure that ethics remain an important focus. For instance, compliance officers no longer report to business unit heads, but directly to risk management in New York. And compensation has been revamped to make pay dependent on corporate-wide results instead of on any one business unit.[43]

New Math

There is today a new calculus of costs and benefits. Costs which were invisible or discounted only a few years ago must now be taken into account if a company is to achieve long-term success. Stakeholders are more aware of the real costs of doing business. No longer can pollution, sloppy ethics, and indifference to the community be assumed to have no cost. Responsible companies minimize these costs in order to maximize profits, not just to accord with local regulations but with their own code of business conduct. The new math is becoming increasingly evident to many members of the media. *Financial Times* editor Jane Fuller, for example, agrees that "taking care of threats to reputation and profits is almost as important as investing to sustain and expand the business."[44]

The worldwide investment community is also beginning to recognize the risk that *not* adhering to a strict set of proactive values will do serious harm to companies, either in stricter regulation, poorer customer relationships, or a diminished ability to attract and retain good people. There is still a long way to go to rebuild confidence in business, even for those companies now embracing an ethics platform and a sense of responsibility to guide business activities and practices. But there are certain rules of engagement that can be instructive for stellar leaders and companies in their efforts to use the power of trust to their advantage.

Checklist for Responsible Profitability

1. **Commitment from the Top.** Top management needs to visibly endorse ethics and responsibility to be certain that they are cascaded into the organization and integrated into decisions. As CEOs become "the face" of their companies, their commitment to strong values increases public trust.

2. **Part of the Company's Mission.** Social costs which were invisible or discounted only a few years ago must now be taken into account. They can only be managed if social values are part of the company's mission.

3. **Reputation Threat.** With the growth in media outlets, corporate actions can no longer be shielded from public view. CEOs must assume that behavior is constantly on display and under scrutiny, and threats to reputation must be taken just as seriously as threats to the commercial operation.

4. **Continuous Training.** While a CEO cannot be aware of the activities and consequences of every employee, it is his or her responsibility to instill certain values and mandate that their violation will not be tolerated.

5. **Recruitment and Retention.** A new generation of employees expects employers to live up to certain standards of behavior and make a positive contribution to the global community. To recruit and retain the best employees, companies have to do more than pay lip service to ethics and corporate citizenship.

6. **Motivation and High Performance.** It is not money that motivates people to get up every day and go to work, but rather their desire to feel they are making a valuable contribution.

7. **Striking a Balance.** Management must gain the trust of a host of stakeholders, including investors, employees, customers, communities, governments, and NGOs, and fulfill its financial and social responsibilities to them.

3

To Tell the Truth

The truth will out.

William Shakespeare,
The Merchant of Venice

*There wasn't a question about how much
disclosure. The answer is 100 percent disclosure.*
Arthur O. Sulzberger Jr., Publisher,
The New York Times[2]

FOR SOME REASON, evolution has provided us the instinct to deflect blame and allow another person to take the consequences. What makes it so difficult for people in power to admit it when something has gone seriously wrong? It happens every day, so it must be an innate human frailty.

Admitting publicly that a mistake has been made is always difficult, and usually embarrassing, too. It takes an exceptionally strong individual to not be tempted—at least momentarily—to conceal or deny bad news. We all know of instances when leaders have found it more expedient to give in to the temptation to step away from mistakes, particularly when any hint of problems is likely to result in an immediate hit on the company's stock price. The problem with avoidance, of course, is that, particularly in today's twenty-four-hour news cycle, any error or lapse is likely be revealed sooner rather than later.

Leaders who are most resilient in the face of trouble tend to carve bold and creative leadership moments out of mistakes and problems. By relying on the power of trust, these leaders touch all major stakeholders in an effort to tell them the unvarnished truth about a crisis as quickly as it is discovered. Being aboveboard is its own reward. When leaders show that they are dealing to the best of their ability with negatives, public opinion about their organization turns sympathetic surprisingly quickly. Stakeholders are much more upset when confronted with subterfuge about bad news than they are about the news itself.

Consider the case of American International Group (AIG), which in May 2005 had to restate $3.9 billion of reported profit because of accounting issues. Chairman and CEO Maurice R. Greenberg famously declared that the scrutiny of regulators was turning "foot faults into murder charges."[1] He failed to recognize that the market was no longer valuing techniques that boost a stock price at any cost.

Executives ignore this new reality at their own peril. After Greenberg was forced to resign, Frank Zarb, the new chairman, understood full well that developing trust and transparency had to be his first order of business. "This company is committed to working openly, without reservation," Zarb declared at his first annual meeting. To show he was serious about doing everything possible to regain the trust of its shareholders, he created several internal advisory groups to carefully review all financial transactions.[2]

Pipeline of Information

The first step toward establishing an atmosphere of trust is to create a pipeline of information that will allow the person at the top to receive bad news—good news, too, for that matter—quickly and unfiltered. The worst-case scenario for leaders who want to adhere to openness and transparency is to be blindsided by negatives that threaten their core business. Yet in many organizations, there is no system in place to ensure that the person at the top is receiving a constant flow of the information most critical to making key decisions. According to a 2005 survey conducted by the Society for Human Resource Management, fewer than half (46 percent) of 347 human resource professionals surveyed reported that their firms collect employee feedback, even on mistakes reported by customers.[3] Even more alarming, a 2004 survey of 459 companies with sales over $250 million conducted by the accounting firm KPMG revealed that 65 percent of employees did not report misconduct that they actually observed.[4] According to a study by the Ethics Resource Center, the oldest nonprofit in the United States devoted to organizational ethics, the top reasons for not reporting misconduct are "the belief that no corrective action would be taken" and "the fear that the reports would not be kept confidential."[5]

Two-way internal communication is crucial to creating an environment in which leaders thrive. Like other elements that foster trust, this no longer can be treated as a luxury, something nice to do when business is good but something that can be jettisoned during a downturn. A formalized, open, quantifiable method of internal communication, with rewards for participation (even if it's just public praise) and no punishment for revealing negatives, will prevent small problems from mushrooming into company-threatening disasters.

In exploring how to manage mistakes of a magnitude that can derail a business or cause the ousting of top management, lessons can be learned from both highly visible successes and well-known failures. In every case, the most critical factors leading to each denouement were the attitude and actions taken by the leader at the top. It is this person's decisions and attitudes that can feed a crisis or turn it into an opportunity to demonstrate leadership in the face of hardship.

All the Truth That's Fit to Print

With a few exceptions, most people and businesses don't set out to be secretive or untruthful. Most have aspirations to realize the

highest levels of quality in their products. Many have elaborate systems set up to catch errors before they reach the customer, the most
celebrated being the Six Sigma formula made famous by Jack Welch
at General Electric. At a minimum, the new Sarbanes-Oxley law requires all publicly held companies to establish internal reporting
controls aimed at preventing fraud. But while these kinds of controls
may work fine with products and accounting tasks, it is infinitely
more difficult to implement them in a people business. People doing
things right are what builds customer trust and loyalty. The difficulties that can arise from mishandling mistakes are particularly acute
in businesses that must rely on people to add value to their product.
Trust, once lost, can be incredibly difficult to regain.

In the newspaper business, trust in what is printed is a core attribute of success. This is certainly true at *The New York Times,* long
considered the gold standard of news and the place where the best
journalists aspire to work. As a result, when chairman and publisher
Arthur Sulzberger Jr. learned that *Times* reporter Jayson Blair had
repeatedly fabricated sources, made up facts, and plagiarized from
other news stories, he knew that the continued credibility of his family's newspaper rested on his response.

"It was particularly painful at an institution like the *Times,*
where a family has shepherded an institution through tough times
and good times," says Sulzberger, who found strength in his family's
history with the company. "Each one of my predecessors faced his
own moments," he recalls. "Whether it was my father with the Pentagon Papers, when his own lawyers said if you print this we will not
defend you, or my grandfather, who went through the Great Depression and World War II, they all faced bad times and made critical decisions that resulted in the *Times* emerging as the preeminent paper
in New York City."[6]

First, Manage Yourself

The public story of how the *Times* responded to the fabrication
of news stories by Jayson Blair is well known, famously divulged on

its own front page. Less well known, but equally enlightening for other leaders, is Sulzberger's thought process leading to the paper going public with its own mistakes.

Sulzberger was out of town when he first heard about the Jayson Blair situation and initially did not think it would become a serious problem. Perhaps he was engaged in a bit of wishful thinking. "There's no question that those who are in business—anyone who is in charge of an institution—has a natural defensiveness," he says. "But any reporter who's been falsifying his or her information is a major problem. More than that, it hurts the fundamentals of what you're in the business of doing. But in those very early days I didn't realize the depth of the issue."

It would take months before the full extent of the scandal was revealed. Blair had stolen or made up all or parts of at least thirty-six articles during a six-month period. The details of the affair made it clear that the *Times*'s internal system of checks and balances was seriously deficient and had allowed the scandal to continue undetected. In one story, a profile of the mother of a soldier in the Iraq war, Blair had made it seem as though he had provided a sympathetic ear for the woman's pain, when in reality he had plagiarized from a story that had appeared in the *San Antonio Express News* written by Macarena Hernandez.[7] In another assignment, in which Blair covered the Washington sniper case, colleagues at the *Times* almost immediately disputed the legitimacy of Blair's reporting and believed he had concocted events and quotations. Similarly, Blair's article about wounded soldiers raised the suspicions of editors at the *Times* and government officials. It turned out that Blair had never even visited the National Naval Medical Center in Bethesda, Maryland, the setting for the story.

What continues to haunt Sulzberger most is Blair's coverage of the Jessica Lynch story.[8] After Lynch's rescue, Blair published several articles about her homecoming, set in her hometown of Palestine, West Virginia. After it became clear that Blair had made factual errors about the Lynch family, falsified encounters with individuals, and lifted quotations from an Associated Press story, Lynch's father was asked why he hadn't called the *Times* after reading so many errors. "Blair describes [the farm] all wrong because he was never there," Sulzberger explains. "The family never called because, the father said, 'I just thought that's what journalists do.' That was just devastating to me. That's *not* what journalists do, and it's *certainly* not what *New York Times* journalists do, although they did in this case, obviously." (Arthor Sulzberger Jr. in discussion with author, June 2005.)

Tell the Truth, Change the Game

As soon as the scope of the problem became known—within a few hours—Sulzberger knew he wanted to put in place fundamental changes. "The thing about the Blair episode is that it was so egregious that it was a little hard to pretend it didn't happen. We couldn't escape it, so it gave us an opportunity to address issues beyond Jayson Blair that go to the very heart of how newsrooms are managed. Quick, full disclosure is only the first step toward solving the problem."

Sulzberger determined that his first priority had to be to move swiftly to reveal the extent of Blair's fabrications and false reporting. "First and foremost, get it out," he recalls thinking. "Get the news out. Get it out yourself. There's nothing worse than a death by a thousand cuts. If you think you're going to be able to hide it, you're fooling yourself if it's a problem of any magnitude. So get ahead of the story and accept the fact that it will be hard, but you will get credit for it."

The *Times* investigated itself and ran a substantive exposé of the problems in the newsroom that had led to Blair's fraudulent reporting. "We put some of our finest journalists on the task of uncovering *ourselves* what had gone wrong," says Sulzberger. "When Howell Raines [former editor in chief who eventually lost his job as a result of the investigation] made the decision not to read the piece before it ran in the paper, that was a leadership moment for us."

Making Fundamental Changes in a Mission-Driven Culture

Just as important as full disclosure was changing the reporting structure in the newsroom that allowed the Blair affair to occur in the first place. Sulzberger knew that Blair wasn't the problem, that he was only a symptom. "How did Jayson get away with this?" Sulzberger wondered. "What was wrong with our systems? We had senior editors saying that Jayson should stop writing even before he became a national correspondent, and yet he was allowed to continue. Why weren't our senior editors talking to each other?"

Sulzberger realized that to correct the kind of problem that could destroy trust in the newspaper on the part of both readers and employees, he had to himself understand why competent, intelligent, caring people could allow errors to multiply until they became impossible to ignore. He knew that fundamental changes were necessary because he couldn't be certain that the paper's staff would be able to put out a quality product if management didn't root out and change the organizational weaknesses that had allowed the scandal to occur in the first place.

Sulzberger explains that fundamental change is particularly difficult in a mission-driven culture. "Every day the newsrooms of America recreate their product," he says. "All the stories are different. The pictures are different. The play is different. Think of how many businesses actually have to do that every day. Every day we have to come up with (effectively) a new drug. So you've got an immensely pressure-filled profession—incredibly smart people, not making a lot of money, quite frankly, in the great scheme of things. They do it because they love it and that builds a sense of being mission-driven. The mission comes first. To get the news out through journalism is no small mission, protected by the First Amendment of the Constitution of the United States. But any structure like that is very hard to change. Think of the army, another mission-driven organization with a great mission: protecting society. Think about emergency rooms, another culture with a great mission: saving lives.

Studies have shown that those three cultures, the army, the emergency room, and the newsroom are more similar to each other than to any other culture. Mission-driven cultures like these are very hard to change."

One of Sulzberger's first moves was to replace the editor in chief, Howell Raines. In an effort to be more timely, oversight of reporters had grown lax. Sacrificing quality for speed occurs in many industries facing competitive pressures, but that doesn't make it acceptable, particularly at a company where trust is implicit in its mandate. Sulzberger knew that restoring the paper's venerated culture, which made top-quality reporting a priority, would take much more than replacing the editor in chief. Raines was a good man, a great newspaperman, under whose watch a system for constantly overseeing the quality of reporting had eroded. Sulzberger's responsibility was to ensure that reporting standards were brought back up to the level that had earned the paper its reputation in years past. His job was complicated by the fact that as in any long-lasting organization, and particularly in one that is mission-based, some values, traditions, and standards are valuable and should be maintained at the same time changes are made.

Assistant managing editor Al Siegal was asked to lead a committee to investigate the root causes of the mistakes that had allowed Blair's fraudulent reporting to go undetected. It was composed of *Times* editors and reporters, but also outsiders, including the former head of the Associated Press and the former ombudsman of *The Washington Post*.

The idea of going through a process of "open inquiry" was not universally endorsed, but Sulzberger insisted, noting that journalists always asked this of others but rarely imposed it on themselves. He did not want a blue-ribbon commission that would write a report that would be scrupulously ignored. "The Siegal Committee met with many of our folks and with me on the record," says Sulzberger. "We vowed to publish their findings, whatever they were, and we did. But more than that, we accepted their findings and made significant changes in how we operate."

The committee had full rein to explore the changes that were needed, resulting in "some real fundamental, institutional changes" that made for "an immensely better news organization," says Sulzberger. "They included changes in the command-and-control structure of the newsroom, the way our editors relate to each other, the way we use human resources, and the hiring of our first-ever public editor, Dan Okrent, responsible for responding to reader questions and comments." The report recommended limiting anonymous sources and explaining why they had to be kept anonymous, reducing factual errors, and making a clearer distinction between news and opinion. It also suggested that the paper's operations and decisions be made more transparent, and that one way to do that was to post interview transcripts on the newspaper's Web site.

Sulzberger has taken to heart the recommendation in the Siegal Report that "an open-door policy is not enough." He insists that "desk heads and masthead editors (the paper's news management) should regularly make themselves available to rank-and-file employees during office hours and staff meetings. All staff members must have avenues to communicate up, down, and horizontally, and to break through the silo mentality." Executive editor Bill Keller, hired to replace the ousted Howell Raines, promised to "hardwire these guidelines into the newsroom and explain them to staff and enforce them."[9]

Sulzberger has taken an aggressive approach to ensuring hands-on management of reporters, those most responsible for the quality of the product. "The Siegal Report is a sound blueprint for the next stage of our campaign to secure our accuracy, fairness, and accountability," says Sulzberger. Today, managers are evaluated and promoted based on their ability to coax out quality reporting, as well as to help reporters turn out stories on deadline. A system of formally scheduled meetings among department heads is intended to prevent another Jayson Blair from being continually promoted even as multiple bosses learned not to trust him. A new standards editor now safeguards the paper's integrity by arbitrating differences between departments on quality and ethical standards and "reinforcing the authority of copy editors to push back in case of unsound practices."[10] Most importantly, the standards editor is responsible for helping department heads create tracking systems for patterns of errors to root out troublemakers before the problems they cause become serious.

The Power of Candor

Very few companies have upper-level people—like the *Times*'s newly created standards editor—whose only job is to help people pursue the truth. All companies, not just the media, would do well to institutionalize the value of honesty *before* a scandal forces them to act. It is important to value the truth tellers, not punish them. Former GE chairman Jack Welch calls the lack of candor among employees "the biggest dirty little secret in business." Even if cover-ups and lies don't create scandal, they result in politicking, bureaucracy, and false politeness that, in Welch's experience, get in the way of surfacing ideas, moving the organization quickly, and preventing inefficiency. So how do you get your people to value truth? Welch recommends, "You reward it, praise it, and talk about it. You make public heroes out of people who demonstrate it. Most of all, you yourself demonstrate it in an exuberant and even exaggerated way—even when you are not the boss."[11]

Sulzberger acknowledges that prior to the changes implemented at the suggestion of the Siegal Report, the *Times* had gradually succumbed to a star system in which reporters tended to be pigeonholed as either stars on the rise or . . . everyone else. That helps no one, including the stars who might be promoted before they are ready. To combat this syndrome, a new position, career development editor, was created. It was filled by an experienced journalist—not an HR person—whose sole responsibility is to "nurture talent" throughout the organization. At the same time, the new editor is responsible for creating "tangible consequences for underperformance."[12]

Changes were also made in reporting standards. The *Times* now enforces much stricter guidelines on the use of unidentified sources, aimed at acknowledging "an understanding that anonymously attributed stories often lack credibility with readers."

Sulzberger has also learned that the way to detect potentially company-shaking errors while they are still small enough to manage is simply to "get out of your cocoon and talk to more people. Widen your network immediately. Start getting your information from a much broader group of sources. I've become more involved at lower levels to stay in touch with what's going on in the newsroom, not relying as much as I used to on just hearing from top editors."

Prior to the Blair affair, Sulzberger had been largely unaware of growing anger and a feeling of malaise on the newsroom floor. A fractious staff meeting at Loews Astor Plaza Theater in Manhattan shortly after the story broke opened his eyes. He told the Siegal Committee that while he knew there were anxieties in the newsroom, the depth of anger and frustration "stunned" him. He acknowledged that he "should have been listening harder to what was happening in the newsroom."[13]

Sulzberger's behavior has changed, and he's a better leader for it. "Once a month I now have a lunch with the entire masthead [all the top editors]. We never did that in the past. In fact, the first time the masthead editors got together in God knows how many years was during the crisis, when I called them together to discuss what we were going to do. I was surprised to discover they had never met as a group. They do now, once a week." Sulzberger also began to encourage e-mail contact from people at lower levels who might notice problems, and the paper's management training program has been greatly expanded.

Commitment to a Different Way of Operating

With a new process in place for reviewing reporting, Sulzberger took another bold step by publicly questioning the newspaper's coverage of weapons of mass destruction (WMD) in Iraq. Articles seeming to support the contentions of the Bush administration that Iraq had them had appeared mostly in 2002 under the byline of veteran *Times* reporter Judith Miller, who had recently been part of a team that won a Pulitzer Prize for its coverage of terrorism. Among other claims about the existence of WMD, she had asserted, based primarily on the word of anonymous informants, that Saddam Hussein had ordered aluminum tubes that could be used to develop nuclear material and had chemical weapons labs hidden in trailers.[14] Had WMD been found in Iraq, no one would have questioned these articles. But after the war began, no such weapons could be found, and Miller's stories, along with those of other reporters, were given a second look.

In May 2004 the editors at the *Times* published a critique of its earlier coverage, pointing out that its Siegal guidelines cautioning against the use of anonymous sources had not been in place when Miller was reporting on Iraq. "We have found a number of instances of coverage that [was] not as rigorous as [it] should have been," it concluded. "In some cases, information that was controversial then, and seems questionable now, was insufficiently qualified or allowed to stand unchallenged. The problematic articles shared a common feature. They depended, at least in part, on information from a circle of Iraqi informants, defectors and exiles bent on 'regime change' in Iraq, people whose credibility has come under increasing public debate."[15]

Mistakes as Opportunities

Getting these problems out on the table has been Sulzberger's way of moving the *Times* to a higher level of reporting standards. If you can't avoid taking heat for a problem, Sulzberger recommends that you simply take your medicine. Don't try to wiggle out of trouble or be less than truthful because it won't help. The truth will eventually find a way to reveal itself. "Just hunker down and start changing the things that caused the problem in the first place," he suggests.

"The hardest thing," says Sulzberger, "is how hard it is for how long. You could never get ahead of this story. There's no time to waste. In retrospect, for example, during that period I should have had a daily morning meeting with the key people, including human resources and public relations."

The Jayson Blair and Judith Miller affairs, as well as Sulzberger's subsequent actions, put the spotlight on the need for the press to be vigilant about its own standards for accuracy, the need to admit errors when they occur, and to make an effort to reawaken or instill journalistic ethics at all levels of a media organization. "We asked ourselves, 'Could that happen here,'" recalls Douglas Clifton, editor of the Cleveland *Plain Dealer*. "The answer is yes; I think it could happen anywhere."[16]

Many news organizations have felt compelled to follow the *Times*'s example and go public with their own sins—and put into place the kinds of controls they hope will prevent similar incidents from occurring. (Shortly afterward, *The Washington Post* followed suit, criticizing its own coverage of the existence in Iraq of WMDs.) Jack Kelley, a foreign correspondent at *USA Today*, was immediately fired when his fabrications of stories were discovered. After his departure, further complaints about Kelley's articles poured in, which later prompted the paper to bring in three experienced external editors to oversee and review the matter.

These very public disclosures, however, haven't prevented other newspapers from experiencing similar problems. Even the sex columnist at the *Vancouver Sun* was terminated for plagiarizing a *New York Times* column. And in July 2005, Jim DeFede of *The Miami Herald* was fired for tape-recording the ramblings of a distraught politician who later committed suicide in the newspaper's lobby. Taping without the subject's permission is illegal in Florida. DeFede's firing was controversial within the news industry. Some argued that an adequate message of censure might have been conveyed to the staff with a long, unpaid suspension, coupled with retraining. But a zero-tolerance policy, if communicated to the staff of any company, can concentrate employees' minds exquisitely on desired ethical behavior.[17]

Sulzberger's actions have helped him in the process of reestablishing trust in *The New York Times* and its practices, and have led

the way toward a renewed commitment among the journalist community to reach higher standards in accurate reporting. Concerned
about lax ethics among editors and reporters, the newspaper industry, under the auspices of the American Society of Newspaper Editors, is investigating whether college journalism students are given a
sufficiently solid ethics education.

The Obfuscation of Others

The New York Times's actions stand out in contrast to those of
many other organizations that instead have relied on obfuscation
and denial to extricate themselves from a problem. While *The New
York Times* responded to the flawed reporting by Blair and Judy
Miller by making a full disclosure of what had happened and by instituting fundamental changes to prevent a recurrence, there have,
unfortunately, been many other management teams that have not
stepped up to evaluate and reveal problems once uncovered. These
examples can be equally instructive.

At the BBC, for example, an apparent lack of a strong commitment to transparency ultimately led to the forced resignations of
those at the head of that news organization. The BBC faced criticism
of its reporting on a British government report on WMDs in Iraq.
Andrew Gilligan, the BBC reporter covering the story, admitted that
his research did not back up the claims in his broadcast that officials
had "sexed up" the report with information they knew to be false.
But when the news corporation was criticized by other news outlets
and British officials for inaccurate reporting, Richard Sambrook, director of news at the BBC, insisted that the news giant had reported
the information correctly. Even after a government inquiry concluded that the BBC had overstated claims that the prime minister
had intentionally influenced intelligence reports, Gilligan remained
steadfast about the overall veracity of the reporting.

The significance of the story depends on whether you choose to
believe the British government's version of events. But what was
clear was that a commission of inquiry found the BBC guilty of

"twisting or falsifying the supposed news to fit a journalist's opinion about where the truth really lies."[18] As a result, its exemplary eighty-year history was tarnished, not because a reporter got a story wrong, but because the news organization was seen as unwilling to thoroughly investigate its own reporting. Those responsible for airing the story were condemned by Lord Hutton, who headed the government inquiry, for defective management and editorial systems, but also for their behavior after the news stories provoked so much controversy. The resignations of BBC director general Greg Dyke and Gavin Davies, the chairman of governors, could quite possibly have been avoided if the BBC had quickly investigated its reporter's actions and made its findings public.

The Reserves Scandal at Shell

Top management at Royal Dutch Shell provides another example of a group that during this decade paid the price for failing to step forward vigorously enough to deal with a significant error in the statement of its oil reserves. An oil company's fundamental value is measured by its reserves. Yet when Royal Dutch Shell found itself facing a crisis, based on an alleged overstatement of the company's reserves, it failed to disclose the news for more than a year.[19]

When in 2001 Sir Philip Watts was promoted from head of exploration to chairman, he immediately commented optimistically about the robustness of the company's oil reserves. This was despite the fact that later reports cited that the overbooking of reserves had reportedly accelerated while Sir Philip had been head of exploration and production.[20]

At least as far back as early 2002, internal memos showed that there were discussions within the company about the possible overstatement of its reserves. One of these memos, written by the new exploration director, Walter van de Vijver, said that he was "tired of lying" about reserves. In subsequent reports in 2002 and 2003, he continued to raise issues with reserve estimates. Reserves are crucial to the outlook and performance of an oil company, yet there was apparently no effort made during this period to disclose the problem. In fact, the audit committees of both Shell boards (the company has a dual company and board structure) received a routine briefing on reserves in October 2003, but did not receive any indication that there was a problem.

It wasn't until early January 2004, in a conference call to analysts and the media, that the board was notified that the oil reserve estimates had been substantially overstated. But Shell chairman Sir Philip Watts didn't even participate in the call. Instead he allowed the company's investor relations' manager to deliver the news. The absence of top management presence illustrated the company's reluctance to take charge of any errors and correct the problem. It is difficult for any board to support a management team that allows an error of this magnitude to occur and then does not take responsibility for informing key stakeholders. Several weeks later Sir Philip was asked to step down.

In the wake of the ensuing scandal, Royal Dutch Shell was forced to restate its oil reserves five times. It was investigated by both U.S. and British regulators, and settled for a record fine of nearly $150 million for having misled investors.[21]

As observers noted at the time, this case was not about people lying to enrich themselves. What emerged was a more subtle motivation, one to which many executives are susceptible. "There was ego at stake," noted Patience Wheatcroft of *The Times* of London. "And that is often valued more highly than cash." Sir Philip Watts had created what *The Times* called "one man's fiefdom," a culture in which making the numbers was everything. "It could happen in any organization which is headed by a strong man surrounded by those who will not challenge him."[22]

Merck in Crisis Mode

Failure to admit an error and perceived attempts at a cover-up can lead stakeholders to believe that management acted with malice. In 2004, the pharmaceutical company Merck took its osteoarthritis drug Vioxx off the market. But as early as February 1997 one Merck researcher had written an internal memo stating that Vioxx created the "possibility of increased cardiovascular events."[23] In September 2001 the Food and Drug Administration told Merck it was marketing Vioxx improperly, concluding that the company had not adequately represented the drug's safety profile. Two years later a study by Harvard's Brigham and Women's Hospital in Boston found that Vioxx had a higher risk of heart attacks than Pfizer's competing drug, Celebrex. After Merck finally pulled Vioxx off the market, a *Lancet* medical journal study claimed the drug might have led to 140,000 cases of serious cardiovascular disease in the United States.[24] The FDA agreed that the product was linked to cardiovascular events, and critics claimed that the company had known this for years but neglected to take action or inform physicians and patients.

The crisis should not have come as a surprise to Merck's top management. Suspicions that management may have known about the possibility of increased risk of death from Vioxx were exacerbated by Chairman and CEO Ray Gilmartin's company's perceived lack of a commitment to open communications. Gilmartin was rarely seen even by those working for Merck, where he was referred to as the "Invisible Man"[25] by some employees. His personal reluctance to step forward and demonstrate transparency increasingly became a problem as the company lurched from one difficulty to the next, suffering from more than the Vioxx issue as it faced patent expirations of significant parts of its product line, slowing growth, and the need for substantial workforce reductions. As Carol Hymowitz wrote in *The Wall Street Journal*, "objecting to bad news doesn't make it go away . . . it only causes spiraling problems."[26]

Gilmartin's disappearing act continued during Merck's first court case associated with Vioxx, brought by the family of a fifty-nine-year-old triathlon athlete who claimed that Vioxx contributed to his death. "Gilmartin did not testify in person, but only by a videotaped statement," recalls one juror. "The big guys didn't show up . . . that didn't sit well with me. Most definitely an admission of guilt."[27]

Indeed, the court found Merck liable and awarded the patient's widow $253 million, reduced to $26 million in accordance with liability limits in Texas.[28] Making matters worse, the Merck board that same week approved generous golden parachutes for two hundred executives. Investors were furious, and by mid-2005 the stock's price had slid 60 percent, Gilmartin had left the company, and more than four thousand patients had filed lawsuits.[29] Estimates of Merck's potential liability range from $2 to $20 billion.[30]

Certainly one important factor that put Merck in such hot water was that management was too disengaged to see that its actions were destroying trust among an important group of new stakeholders—potential jury members. The public trial in Texas shifted attention from the facts and what the science showed to anger rooted in mistrust caused by a perceived lack of honesty. One juror summed up the company's predicament when he said, "Respect us, that's the message."[31]

Seizing the Leadership Moment

There are numerous examples of organizations that have failed to admit their mistakes or refused to discuss problems openly, including well-known companies which over the years have earned and sustained good reputations as valued corporate citizens. During the past decade there has been greater visibility and seemingly higher numbers of executives who have cut corners or made significant errors in judgment. Indeed, earnings restatements of publicly held companies have soared during the past decade, from 59 in 1997, to 195 during the first six months of 2005. This demonstrates a real need for greater vigilance and a growing recognition of the need for truth telling.[32]

The temptation to hide the truth never entirely goes away, especially in the face of a full-blown media-driven crisis. Leaders must decisively take responsibility for errors as soon as they occur, no matter the consequences. It's not just that problems *always* get worse when ignored, denied, or swept under the rug, although that's certainly true. But it goes beyond the obvious. "The buck stops here" didn't make Harry Truman's reputation because it was a philosophy that prevented problems from being exacerbated by neglect. It made his reputation because the public recognized it as a signature of leadership. According to Harvard professor Rosabeth Moss Kanter, "people associated with winning streaks are unlikely to create negative perceptions when they admit flaws before being forced to do it. Indeed, the opposite occurs: Others think more of them for being big enough to assume responsibility."[33]

"Churchill said, 'If you're candid about your mistakes, that's the beginning of self-correction,'" adds Bob Hormats of Goldman Sachs. "The first part of wisdom is to understand your mistakes and to admit them. If you're not candid, what's the incentive to change?"

"We make mistakes, sometimes even big mistakes," explains Daniel Vasella of Novartis. "We get it wrong. In this respect, you have to be honest, but more importantly you have to be honest with yourself—to your conscience, your bizarreness, weaknesses and exceptionalities as parts of your own personality. If you can face this, knowing that nobody is perfect, you can also face the outside world."

Taking charge, admitting mistakes fully and quickly, is difficult because it goes against human nature. It takes courage and leadership to get ahead of a problem and commit to prompt full disclosure. It is also the only way to survive and to move forward with strength.

CHECKLIST FOR TRUTH TRUMPS CRISES

1. **Enforce full disclosure.** First and foremost, get the news out. Get it out yourself. Learn Sulzberger's lesson: "There's nothing worse than a death by a thousand cuts. If you think you're going to be able to hide a problem of any magnitude, you're fooling yourself. So get ahead of the story and accept the fact that it will be hard." If you are up front from the beginning, and responsive to problems, "the worst" will be considerably easier to handle than if you stonewall until you are forced into change.

2. **Reach out to key constituencies.** Consider each of your key stakeholder groups and know how you can meet their diverse needs. During the Jayson Blair scandal, stakeholders included the *Times* board of directors and the Sulzberger family. But they also included the newsroom, which was going through a crisis of the heart, and the paper's readership, which also had reason for concern. Sulzberger understood the importance of reaching out to all these groups.

3. **Widen your network.** Before you can get ahead of a problem or crisis, be sure of your facts. That requires extending your contacts deep into the company. Don't rely exclusively on your usual sources or your direct reports. Listen to people at all levels of the organization. "The best commanding generals spend a great deal of time talking to privates,"[34] notes Rice University professor of management Duane Windsor.

4. **Encourage the internal reporting of negative news.** Begin a process which encourages reporting of negative news and allows you to learn of problems promptly. Leaders can't admit mistakes if they have no knowledge that a mistake has been made. "The leader is the last to know" is an operating principle at far too many organizations. There is a natural human tendency to present only good news to the boss. Systems can be put in place to ensure that awareness of company problems reaches the executive level quickly.

5. **Be patient and persistent.** Make peace with the idea that an error of any major consequence will have an impact on top management for an extended period of time. "While the speed with which things move is extraordinary and relentless, even more difficult is the second part, that is, even when it is over, it's not really over for top management," says Sulzberger.

6. **Seize the opportunity to make fundamental changes.** Reacting to a major mistake provides a chance to dig down to the problems that allowed it to occur in the first place and to make fundamental changes in systems and processes that will ensure quality. How and why could it happen? Who knew what when, and what steps should they have taken immediately? "Blair was the canary for the mine," says Sulzberger. "The problem went much deeper than Jayson, was much more fundamental, and that's what had to be addressed long-term."

7. **Capture the leadership moment.** Leaders embody the values of an organization. It is critical that they speak out, are visible, take responsibility, and then begin the process of restoring trust and confidence. You'll be astonished at what a difference putting a face on a problem—the face of the head of the organization—makes during times of crisis, and during good times, too.

4

Seizing Opportunity from Disaster

A journey of a thousand miles begins with a single step.[1]

Attributed to Confucius

We are going to stay focused on responsible perfor-
mance. This is a multiyear, forever type thing, not a
one-trick pony for a year.

Ed Breen,
Chairman and CEO, Tyco[1]

ONE COULD BE excused for concluding that Ed Breen was making an ill-advised career move when he decided to become CEO of Tyco in the summer of 2002. Dennis Kozlowski had just been forced to step down as CEO for dipping into the company's coffers to fund his personal excesses. The press had had a field day with disclosures of Kozlowski's expenditures, highlighted by $6,000 gold shower curtains and multimillion-dollar birthday parties.

Kozlowski became emblematic of highly visible, disgraced CEOs, but it turned out that Tyco had even more serious problems than an indicted, recently departed CEO. During his tenure at Tyco, Kozlowski had spent $63 billion to acquire a hodgepodge of companies, earning him the moniker "Deal-a-Day Dennis." By 2002, it had become clear

GREGORY

*"Now we'll all close our eyes and cover our ears, and the person who took
the four hundred and twenty-eight million dollars will put it back."*

that the combination of these disparate companies wasn't working, and that both investors and customers had lost confidence in the conglomerate.[2] With an $11 billion loan payment coming due, part of $28.1 billion in debt, the company seemed headed for bankruptcy. Even Breen's wife, Lynn, advised him against leaving Motorola, where he had just recently become president and chief operating officer after rising through several senior positions. Breen remembers his wife telling him, "You're kind of crazy. You could be running Motorola for the next twenty years. Why would you make this kind of move?"

It's not as if Breen didn't know that saving Tyco would be a tremendously difficult, some were saying impossible, undertaking. "It wasn't just the scandal," Breen remembers. "The much bigger problem was the company's mounting liquidity crisis." When he asked for monthly profit-and-loss statements for each of the businesses and was told that they did not exist, Breen knew this was a company out of control.

But Breen also saw what others did not: an underlying strength in Tyco. Peeling away the excess, a result of hundreds of acquisitions during the previous five years, Breen could envision a smaller, leaner, more focused company that would take advantage of Tyco's key assets in its core businesses of electronics, health care, and security. "I really tried to dig down into the iceberg to see what was there," he explains. "Looking out over a multiyear period, I thought the company had great opportunities."

Most important from Breen's point of view, he believed *he* was the person to take on the challenge. "From studying the situation,

I felt I could really have a big impact and get it fixed. Once I make that determination, I'm not shy about taking a risk. It seemed exciting."[3]

Some companies hit by criminal charges against their top management fail to survive. (WorldCom and Enron come to mind.) Companies with damaged reputations and without leadership often suffer a "meltdown." In contrast, a strong leader who assumes responsibility for a company in trouble knows instinctively that restoration of trust can be the most important step in beginning the recovery. Breen knew he would have to be patient, that he could be facing a long period of confidence building and that he would have to demonstrate fast that things had changed. Consistently meeting financial targets would be necessary before he could begin to overcome skepticism and regain credibility. For successful leaders, this means establishing trusted relationships with key stakeholders so that expectations are reset both internally and externally and it is clear that everyone in the company is aligned around the same goals.

Breen's First One Hundred Days

Breen wanted to move quickly to restore trust among Tyco's two most important stakeholders. "Number one, I wanted to show employees that fundamental change was coming and that we intended to get this thing righted," Breen remembers. "I viewed coming in that if ten thousand sales people around the world were disconnected with their customers or were conveying the idea that the wheel was falling off, the company had no chance. And number two, or maybe it was 1A, our investor base had to be patient, to give us a little time to begin to fix the problems. But for that to happen, they would have to see quick, fundamental change occur during the first one hundred days."

Toward that end, one of Breen's first official acts as CEO was to explain to employees his reasons for joining the company, why he saw great potential, and the basic rules he would institute from day one. In particular, he emphasized:

1. An absolute commitment to integrity and trustworthiness throughout the organization
2. A relentless dedication to creating and enforcing best corporate governance practices
3. A dedication to customer satisfaction by consistently delivering superior products and service
4. A focus on businesses that could become leaders in their industries
5. A recognition that with growth will come new opportunities and a positive work environment for Tyco employees
6. A promise that once these first five goals were attained, Tyco's credibility with each of its constituencies, as well as its shareholder value, would be restored

But Breen knew that it was going to take a lot more than pep talks to employees to bring about the fundamental change that was needed at Tyco. During his first hundred days there, he took some bold steps that demonstrated he was serious. His most dramatic decision was to replace the entire board of directors, as well as 290 of the 300 most senior corporate positions.

"Very quickly we were able to say this was a new company which couldn't be viewed as the Tyco of the past," Breen says, explaining his motives. "In a few months we had rebuilt senior management with what we considered were world-class people."

As another break from the past, Breen traded Tyco's sumptuous corporate headquarters in Manhattan with its pricey views of Central Park for a nondescript office park in Princeton, New Jersey.[4] "If you go through the Princeton headquarters, of the five hundred people, there are maybe ten who were there prior to my arrival," says Breen. "We totally rebuilt every senior corporate direct report until it was a new team."

Breen decided that Tyco had fallen so far that cleaning house was the only way to restore faith in the company. But he was careful to keep a handful of senior management on, plus many more than that in the company's two thousand locations around the world. Bob Hormats of Goldman Sachs cautions against being rash during even the most radical transformation. "Employees know who's good, so if you simply wash everyone out, they don't get a sense that merit means very much," he explains. "By keeping some very good people, Ed Breen reinforced the importance of human assets. The rapid pace of change, but also its perceived fairness, instilled trust among the workforce, which was needed for the difficult days ahead."[5]

Breen is an inspiring example of the kind of executive who can convince reluctant stakeholders to suspend judgment long enough to allow a radically changed business model to begin showing results. That will convince them to stick with management a little longer, until the turnaround is complete. A positive financial performance after the initial changes have had a chance to sink in also helps, of course. In Tyco's case, during the two years prior to June 2005 the company's share price increased 200 percent, debt was reduced from more than $20.4 billion to $14.4 billion, and the ratio of net debt to total capital declined from 41 percent to 27 percent.[6] The rise in value signaled that Breen had set a new course, although the road ahead would have many ups and downs.

Back to Basics

In a situation like Tyco's, a good rule of thumb is that whatever you were doing before disaster struck, do the opposite. This goes be-

Tyco–Ed Breen Becomes Chairman and CEO in July 2002

Five-year monthly stock performance for Tyco

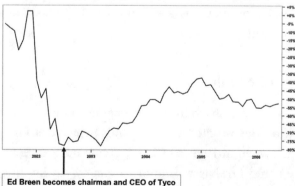

Ed Breen becomes chairman and CEO of Tyco

yond a mere turnaround aimed at getting a wounded company back on its feet. Leaders will want to explicitly and publicly restate their business goals and reset expectations. Yes, it will be disruptive, but you have to break the mold to get employees motivated and restore their morale. If the situation is bad enough, the workforce will no doubt be hoping you'll do just that. By the time such a dramatic turnaround becomes necessary, they will have had all they can take of the uncertainty that comes from bad decisions and a corrupt bureaucracy. In Tyco's case, a sharp turn—not quite as radical as a U-turn—off the disastrous path down which Kozlowski had led the company meant putting a halt to an undisciplined growth strategy that had seen Kozlowski acquire nearly a thousand businesses in a six-year period. "Here was a company," explains Breen, "that was the biggest acquisition machine around. It was almost like a private equity firm. As soon as I got here I announced we were going to become a world-class *operating* company and that we wouldn't be making a single acquisition for at least a few years."

Instead, Breen began a program of divestiture, closing companies that didn't fit with Tyco's main businesses, selling some, and consolidating others. When he arrived, he counted more than 2,100 separate entities that made up Tyco, so there was, in his words, "a lot of low-hanging fruit." After two years, he was still trimming, closing, or selling about fifty businesses, representing $2.1 billion, or 5 percent of its revenues.

Effective sharp turns are not always based on divestiture, of course, or even returning to a focus on a company's core business. Rather, the common denominator is a sharp turn off a disastrous path and a profound need to restore trust.

A Sharp Turn at Renault

You can also jump-start a sharp turn by engaging employees and showing sensitivity to a deep-rooted culture. Louis Schweitzer knew he faced a tough task when in 1999, as CEO of Renault, he invested $5.4 billion to take control of Nissan Motor Company. At the time, Nissan was floundering. For many years it had been struggling to turn a profit and had low visibility in the United States. Among its other problems were too much production capacity and low margins. Renault, too, was considered a global also-ran, and many observers were predicting that the combination of the two companies would mark the death of both.[7]

Schweitzer selected Carlos Ghosn to lead Nissan and manage the turnaround. Ghosn understood the need for creativity if they were going to bring the Japanese automaker back to profitability. As a Brazilian employed by a French company trying to turn around a Japanese automaker, Ghosn decided he couldn't impose a solution from above because he could have been viewed as an outsider who didn't understand the company's underlying culture. Instead, in an effort to figure out what needed to be done, he created cross-functional teams to get "line managers to see beyond the functional or regional boundaries that define their direct responsibilities."[8] The five hundred middle managers involved in this effort, plus two senior-level sponsors, were divided into groups and given three months to review a specific part of an operation and make recommendations. In the end, they recommended changes that were exceptionally radical to the Japanese business culture, including extensive layoffs and closures, selective entry into new markets (such as minicabs in Japan), and strategic investments (such as producing Renaults in Mexico). To control costs, the seniority rule was set aside. Performance was the key factor in an employee's promotion, rather than the more typical Japanese approach of tenure and age. The compensation system, too, was refocused around performance. Responsibilities were clearly delineated, overcoming cultural tendencies to avoid well-defined areas of responsibility for many senior managers.

Again, however, the glue that held it all together was trust. According to Ghosn, "People have to believe that they can speak the truth and that they can trust what they hear from others. Building trust is a long-term project. Those in charge have to demonstrate that they do what they say they'll do, and that takes time."

Ghosn insisted that every report he received was "totally clear and verifiable." He made it equally evident that he expected people to stand by every claim they made. In return, he promised to resign

the first time he broke a promise.[9] Under Ghosn's tenure, Renault
and Nissan have made great strides in profitability, customer accep-
tance, and pride among employees, and investors have taken notice.
Renault's stock price jumped 20 percent during the first nine months
after Ghosn was named chief executive of the parent company, and
another 30 percent between January 2005 and February 2006.

The common thread among companies like Tyco, Nissan, and
many others which managed a sharp turn that took them off a disastrous path is that the top executive of each harnessed the power of
trust. This trust gave them resilience, and bought the time that patience offers to change the mind-set of a company that had lost its way.
They used inspiration to boost profits at a mature company, sometimes
even pulling it away from the brink in the process. Although the problems of each of these companies are diverse and the solutions varied,
by their focused actions their leaders were able to reset the engine of
their growth, inspire employees, and change investor perceptions.
Then with some breathing room, they could begin to write a new story.

Creating a New Blueprint at Tyco

Replacing the entire board of directors and most of the senior
management team was only Ed Breen's first step in Tyco's makeover.
Equally important, obviously, was choosing the right replacements.
"As we rebuilt the team and the board, we tried to think through a
matrix of what talent we needed to rebuild as a world-class operating company," Breen recalls. Breen saw the need to show employees
and the market by who was hired exactly what kind of company Tyco
was becoming.

Hiring people who were excited by mergers and acquisitions obviously wasn't the way to go. One of Breen's earliest new hires, for example, was Bob Frantz, from GE's aircraft engine business, to head
up Tyco's environmental health and safety tasks. Frantz's mission was
to establish company standards, not just to follow the minimum standards of the jurisdictions where Tyco operates. Another was Eric Pillmore, a former coworker of Breen's at Motorola, who was brought in

as senior vice president of corporate governance, a position he still holds at this writing. Pillmore became one of the architects of the company's ethical framework, which aimed at allowing the company to move beyond the lapses of the past and at the same time strengthen its performance. "Given the urgency of the situation," he says, "we felt it was important—in order to establish Ed [Breen] as the leader—to establish a set of values that he believed in. We were advised it would take nine to twelve months for the values to bubble up internally, but we felt it was necessary to get it done more quickly than that."

Those values, now printed on posters all over the company, including on the buildings themselves, are integrity, accountability, teamwork, and excellence. They were communicated in a worldwide twenty-four-city rollout in fifteen languages, all spelled out on the Tyco Web site. Key components were called "Integrity Matters" and "Performance Matters," but specific behaviors, such as "managerial courage" (speaking up at lower levels, responding to feedback at higher levels), were also stressed. "Compensation is not mathematically based on these values, but they definitely affect performance reviews and promotions," says Pillmore.

Pillmore also believes that the way in which the values are driven into the company has a role in their success. In short:

1. Establish values that the leader believes in.
2. Create a guide for ethical conduct to use in training. This should include vignettes and guidelines on what can go wrong.
3. Create and deliver robust training and set rewards to drive the message home.
4. Ask employees and leaders to sign an agreement to uphold the values.[10]

Pillmore notes that in its 2004 proxy, Tyco recommended voting in favor of a shareholder resolution asking the company to assess its corporate-wide environmental management system, a rare gesture of support from a company to its shareholders. "This move exemplifies

Tyco's new attitude toward its stakeholders," says Pillmore. "When we see good ideas, we like to jump on them. I think our employees and our shareholders all had a very strong voice in shaping what we did in 2002 that turned the company around. You can pay a lot of money for consultants to tell you how to do things, or you can go out on the road and talk to shareholders, customers, and employees and get better ideas, if you listen."[11]

Early on, Breen laid out a calendar for the year, scheduling a detailed review of each of Tyco's operating companies. He wanted to personally make sure every leader knew his or her responsibilities. No longer would division heads and other executives be allowed to buy results through an acquisition or overly optimistic projection. "There's no magic to this," Breen admits. In contrast to the laissez-faire management of the past, every other month Breen chairs a disciplined operating review meeting with each business. It includes a review of strategy, capital allocation, and organizational leadership.

Regaining Control with Six Sigma

Under the old Tyco, with hundreds of operating companies, it was nearly impossible to identify key processes in order to set priorities, especially in terms of where to devote resources. As the company became leaner and more focused, Breen pulled what he thought he needed from the process-improvement strategies of Six Sigma. He focused on making Tyco employees understand that each one of them could use Six Sigma to their advantage. As Jack Welch famously wrote, "Once you understand the simple maxim, 'Variation is evil,' you'll be 60 percent of the way to becoming a Six Sigma expert yourself. The other 40 percent is getting the evil out."[12]

During Breen's first year, Tyco trained 2,500 (one in ten) employees to be "green belts" or "black belts" in Six Sigma. The black belts focused on the program full-time and were dispersed into every one of Tyco's businesses around the world, reporting to the operating company presidents. Green belts support the process and help build buzz. Every year, another 2,500 are trained. "It's not easy, it takes time," says Breen, "but we're building traction, so every year it gets better and we get closer to a Six Sigma culture. Over time, you develop a network throughout the company that understands what you're talking about, drives it, and makes it work."

In fiscal 2004 alone, Breen applied the principles of Six Sigma to 1,100 different projects, for a total costs savings of $278 million. Most of it was accomplished by tackling four specific problems:

1. Redundant factories
2. Unnecessary real estate
3. Too little working capital
4. Too many people making purchasing decisions

Breen began with Tyco's far-flung, overlapping factories, aiming to "collapse the footprint very significantly." Criteria were put in place to compare the efficiency of every manufacturing operation. Those factories producing at a cost disadvantage were quickly closed or merged with more efficient facilities. Certain divisions were closed entirely, based on similarly detailed, disciplined guidelines.

Breen used Six Sigma techniques to differentiate those facilities that were producing economies of scale from those that were not, becoming what David Lei and John Slocum Jr. of Cox School of Business at Southern Methodist University call a *consolidator*, a "firm that seeks to maximize the benefits of cost and process efficiencies in their attempt to garner industry-wide economies of scale."[13]

Next, Breen focused on rationalizing Tyco's real estate holdings. Millions of square feet of physical plant were eliminated, seven million in fiscal 2004 alone. Much of this came from closing unneeded or inefficient facilities identified in step one of the process, but a significant portion of the real estate savings also came from recognizing and correcting the excesses of the Koslowski era. Gone is the Manhattan headquarters and quite a few redundant facilities that had become part of Tyco during its acquisition binge. Real estate sales were part of an overall strategy to use brick-and-mortar assets

to their full capacity, without duplication. "It isn't like we're shrinking the company," Breen explains. "Our sales were growing at the
same time we were shrinking the physical plant."

Perhaps the most vital part of Tyco's adaptation of the Six Sigma
umbrella was a program that focused on maximizing working capital. Cash flow increased from $780 million in fiscal 2002 to $3.2 billion in 2003, to about $4 billion in 2004.

Finally, Breen brought Six Sigma to bear in an effort to control
the cost of routine expenditures. The purchase of everything from
telephone service to freight to furniture were consolidated so that all
purchasing decisions were made through Tyco corporate rather
than being sourced dozens of times by dozens of different operating
companies. Volume discounts, operating efficiencies, and other cost
control measures that search out opportunities to become more
streamlined in routine purchases have resulted in annual savings of
about $300 million. Yet it's surprising how few big companies are
willing to take on the complicated logistics (not to mention the lo-
calized howling) to implement these kinds of commonsense profit-
improvement techniques. These are the kinds of simple actions,
though, that make a workforce say, "Finally, somebody in corporate
is wising up," not a bad sentiment for a new leader to cultivate.

Of course, says Breen, some of the operating companies were already operating within fine tolerances and didn't have to make many
adjustments to meet the rigor of Six Sigma. Breen made a particular
effort to gain the trust of the heads of the profit centers by making it
clear they were part of a new Tyco. "We said to them, 'We are going
to stay focused on responsible performance. This is a multiyear, forever type thing, not a one-trick pony for a year." Rather than striving
to integrate acquisition after acquisition as the old Tyco had, employees were being asked to manage the existing companies at peak
efficiency. And they were being asked to make it a way of life.

Building Resiliency Based on Trust

Breen couldn't just assume that the people at Tyco would buy
into his turnaround program. He had to work to show employees

that they could trust him and his ideas, and those of his mostly new lieutenants. "These were big changes we were asking employees to accept, including an entirely new board of directors, president and chairman, and management team," Breen recalls. "But it's amazing how resilient the human spirit is and how they will rally around if they think, 'Hey, we're working toward a fixed goal.' I found that our employees were very resilient when they thought they could see you walking up to the top of the mountain and that positive change was happening."

Breen has talked to tens of thousands of employees in his three years at the company, from top executives to the people farthest down the organization in Tyco's production facilities. The most vital part of this communication effort, he believes, has been a commitment to telling the truth. In his early days as CEO, those on the front lines were perfectly aware that the company was in crisis, and they quite rightly feared for their jobs. They wanted to know from Breen precisely how he would be dealing with the company's liquidity crisis, and in particular whether he would be selling off big pieces of Tyco—places where they worked—just to raise money.

"It's amazing to watch what happens if you're open with people and tell them the real facts," says Breen. "Here's how I'm going to fix it. I don't have all the answers yet, but here's where I'm trying to lead."

Bob Hormats of Goldman Sachs has seen many companies deal with life-or-death struggles. "You really have to change the way employees think about the company, while at the same time you are changing the company itself," he says. "Getting people to think like one company as opposed to a lot of little companies is an enormous task. With Breen, people believed he really wanted to clean up and not make compromises on the fundamentals."

In the retelling, the experience of many CEOs in managing sharp turns makes it seem that the changes they introduced were inevitable. Of course, he invested in a long-shot idea. Of course, she divested businesses that were distracting attention from core competencies. Of course, he created a message that all constituencies could buy into. Of course, he brought in an entirely new management team.

But leaders at all levels know that instituting change is never as easy as it appears in hindsight. The interesting thing is that with trust, you will get backing. Business or division heads in crisis are desperate for a leader, and you will be given a lot of leeway—to either succeed or fail. A long-lasting sharp turn depends, to a great extent, on your ability to convince stakeholders that you have the answers, even if you are not sure yourself. In Breen's case, he knew he could convince stakeholders that the company had turned the corner by delivering positive financial numbers. But he also knew that SEC investigations and class-action lawsuits continued to affect overall perceptions of Tyco. In order to change this, Breen would have to inspire confidence.

Commitment to Transparency and Constant Communications

Among the companies I've observed making sharp turns from a disastrous path, focused, straightforward communication has been fundamental to the success of their transformation. Indeed, Ed Breen believes that communicating, or even overcommunicating, is a crucial ingredient in any successful rebuilding process. The entire company will be looking over your shoulder as you make decisions, so this is not the time to be secretive. It is the time to be fully transparent with your stakeholders. Breen found that the mere act of opening up got people on the same team and started to rebuild camaraderie and a new culture.

Communicating widely and truthfully about every aspect of your proposed transition is something leaders must steel themselves to do. Unfortunately, your instincts will try to lead you in exactly the opposite direction. When you are in the middle of a transition, you'll feel like keeping major changes to yourself until you're sure they're going to work. That's what those running the accounting firm Deloitte & Touche did. After months of public discussion and preparation to become two separate businesses, it was suddenly announced in mid-2003 that the company was not going to spin off its consulting arm after all. Deloitte Consulting's CEO, Paul Robinson, called the result "psychological whiplash" and devastating to the company's 20,000 employees and 5,000 partners "because we had effectively painted a picture for them of an independent consulting company that would have had an exciting image in the market. We communicated that dream so well that almost all our people got behind it." Preparing employees and other stakeholders for the possibility that the spin-off would fail would have limited the damage. "You've spent considerable time, effort, and energy persuading and convincing everybody, including yourself, that the proposition that you're going on is the right answer and the best answer, and then all of a sudden you completely change direction," Robinson recalled months later. "I realized that there's only one thing more difficult than separation, and that's reintegration after you've decided to separate."[14]

Accomplishing that reintegration required an intense effort at communication, says Robinson. "It required us to communicate all the time—about twenty-four hours a day, it seemed." Robinson and other members of top management opened their doors to take the fallout. "Employees wanted to yell at someone, and our executives made themselves available," says Robinson. Conference calls with huge numbers of employees were set up in such a way that employees could ask questions and receive feedback. Robinson feels the totality of the communication effort was one of the factors that has made the new Deloitte Consulting even stronger than the spun-off company would have been. "Just being honest seemed to work extremely well,"[15] he says.

Passion Drives Enthusiasm

Should leaders fall in love with their new business models? Ed Breen of Tyco thinks that's absolutely necessary to keep people on your side. "You've got to have a burning passion for what you're doing," he argues. "When you're in a crisis mode, it is totally all-consuming. You are going to be working long days and weekends, so you've got to have a burning desire to want to do it. Passion is a big thing for a company in crisis. People are going through a lot, whether it's the new management team coming in working seven days a week firefighting, or employees worried about their future."

Embracing change helps leaders deal with the fact that at the end of the day, they're really out there alone. Even those who have come up through the ranks will be making a lot of personnel changes during these critical times. That means they probably won't have trusted advisors around them, at least until the key talent they bring in can become accustomed to working with each other. Even if people have worked together before, crisis strains all relationships. But if you really believe in the changes you are making, you'll be able to withstand a lot of push-back from stakeholders without letting it rattle you.

Don't be afraid to repeat yourself. Every executive and politician knows that by the time you are thoroughly sick of hearing yourself say the same thing over and over, your listeners are just beginning to get it. Say it with slogans and sound bites, internally as well as externally. Yes, people will tell you slogans can be viewed as childish or a pure marketing ploy. But people remember them. Just be certain that the short, clear messages you are sending are in synch with the sharp turn you are trying to maneuver.

Learn to celebrate successes. Celebrations and strict discipline might sound contradictory, but according to Breen they are essential components in any successful turnaround. In a crisis mode, he believes you have to focus on a few priorities. Have a personal list of no more than ten items—preferably fewer—that you allow yourself to pursue. "You can't worry about every brush fire going on around you," says Breen. "If I listened to other people or the press, I'd be overwhelmed with a hundred problems that could distract me. The important thing is to fix the things you absolutely have to fix." By focusing on a few priorities, companies can celebrate progress on those defined goals and get to others later after they've experienced normalization.

But what about the fun? Breen says that fun comes with the territory because as far as he's concerned, nothing is more exciting than meeting a challenge. "I've had a lot of people say to me, 'Ed, in the first year, that was the most fun I've ever had in my career.' It was stressful and tense, but it had a lot of excitement." That's an attitude all executives should cultivate, regardless of whether they are in crisis mode. There is satisfaction in small, and ultimately large, successes. Celebrating these milestones raises morale, creates constructive enthusiasm, and ultimately raises productivity that can be sustained during tough times.

Coming Out the Other Side as a "Normal Company"

Eventually, a sharp turn stops feeling like a roller-coaster ride and more like ordinary striving for results. Tyco has made a lot of progress toward stability and profitability since its radical makeover. But leaders like Breen are reluctant to declare victory. Instead, they know that these changes are a way of life, and will be key to evolving the company toward a focus on operational results and organic growth.

Proof that things are on the right course comes from successfully meeting a series of disciplined goals. In Tyco's case, these goals included reducing debt to $10 billion by using increased cash flow to fix the balance sheet and to buy back stock to create additional shareholder value. "We're getting to where we want to be: a solid investment-grade company,"[16] says Breen, whose latest effort to improve shareholder value is to explore breaking up the company so that each new entity would focus on one of Tyco's three areas of expertise—electronics, health care, and security.[17]

Breen believes that "perhaps the turning point was when we suddenly realized we had stopped firefighting. We're becoming a normal company. Legacy issues are no longer taking up a high percentage of my time." According to Andrew Grove, former CEO of Intel and himself a veteran of sharp turns, "Your way through a strategic inflection point is like venturing into what I call a 'valley of death,' the perilous transition between the old and the new ways of doing business."[18] Breen is just thankful that Tyco was able to move out of the valley, and in record time.

CHECKLIST FOR DRIVING A SHARP TURN

1. **Focus on the basics.** Confidence will be restored only when financial targets are consistently met.
2. **Break with the past.** Whatever you were doing before disaster struck, change the pattern now.
3. **Move fast.** Show some immediate actions, but expect a long period of confidence building.
4. **Change the mind-set.** Be open with employees and tell them the facts. Change the way employees think about the company while you're changing the company itself.
5. **Communicate even the uncertainty.** Don't lose heart or your nerve when reactions are negative as you communicate tough news.
6. **Build trust to gain resiliency.** As a trusted leader, you will be given a lot of leeway—to either succeed or fail. Remember that the glue that holds it all together is trust. People have to believe that they can speak the truth and that they can trust what they hear from top management.
7. **Celebrate milestones, but resist declaring victory.** The team will need to celebrate their progress, but don't cloud the fact that the road will be long. Communicating, or even overcommunicating, exactly what you're doing can be the most important single factor in a successful sharp turn. A new business strategy will only be successful if everyone understands it.

5

Love Thy Enemy:
The Benefits of Taking
Critics Inside

*It takes two to speak the truth—one to speak, and
another to hear.*

Henry David Thoreau[1]

*Say to people this is what I'm going to do, have a
debate, listen, then go ahead.*

Lord John Browne, CEO, BP[2]

ENVIRONMENTALISTS HAD ALREADY been talking for years about the
perils of global warming when in 1995 Lord John Browne became
CEO of what was then known as British Petroleum. Less than two
years later, during a speech in Stanford in 1997, he made a dramatic
announcement that shook the oil industry. Speaking before a group
of executives at Stanford Business School, Browne became the first
oil company executive to concede that there was enough evidence to
conclude that global warming was a reality—and that his company
was contributing to it. He pledged to cut BP's own greenhouse emissions by 10 percent.

Browne's speech was a shock to those in the industry and to many within BP. "He had the nerve to make a change," says Nick Butler, BP's group vice president of strategy and policy development. "About 60 percent of the company thought he was wrong, some very actively."[3] Many in the industry labeled him a heretic. "The API [American Petroleum Institute] told me that I'd left the church," Browne remembers.[4] At the time Browne made his announcement BP itself was a member of both the API and the Global Climate Coalition, both of which were minimizing the seriousness of global warming.

These were no extemporaneous, off-the-cuff remarks by Browne, but rather a well-thought-out strategy after a long period of contemplation. Shortly after taking over the helm of BP Browne determined that he would dig into the facts and meet with critics to shape his own thoughts on climate change and the role the oil industry had in it. He believed BP had a responsibility not to put its head in the sand. "We're in this as part of society," he said.[5]

While others in the industry did not consider global warming to be a legitimate concern, Browne decided he had a duty to investigate the facts and come to his own conclusions. He began to seriously consider the weight of evidence as it grew and the opinion of those in the company who felt BP had an indefensible position. At the very least, he understood that critics could interfere with the company's ability to do business and that he had a responsibility to shape BP's response to those who decried BP's impact on the environment. Just as the major tobacco companies were eventually forced to confront the facts about the healthfulness of their products, so too were the major oil companies eventually going to have to face the reality of their business. The difference was that Browne was adamant that BP would be proactive, take the lead, and determine the right position on climate change.

Browne credits a "deep dive" into the physics of global warming, in consultation with dozens of scientists, as a driving factor in shaping his opinion. He was helped by a close relationship with Eileen Claussen, president of the Pew Center on Global Climate Change, and by other nonprofits, including the Environmental Defense Fund. Talking to these groups and others—all of them vocal critics of oil industry policy—made Browne realize that BP needed to adopt a new platform on climate change. He was certain that this had to be elevated to a priority topic for the company, that it was something that would continue to grow in importance and gain momentum with consumers and governments.[6]

Browne jumped over the sticking point that makes dealing with critics so difficult for many organizations: a reluctance to even admit that there could be a cause for complaint. Because he did so early on in the argument over global warming, BP was able to concentrate on demonstrating to the majority of stakeholders that its commitment to more responsible business practices was more than just window dressing. Browne was able to cascade responsible actions throughout the corporation and its supply chain. Slowly, sometimes painfully, he created a new vision of BP, embedding new values in the organization and rewarding those willing to help him achieve them. "We did it to get a seat at the table, to be able to discuss validly with people how this would impact our industry," says Browne. "I think we've had some impact on how the oil industry thinks about these things."[7]

Everyone's a Critic

As the pace of information spread increases, and the number of activist nongovernmental organizations soars, companies are well advised to pay attention to their critics. Given the rise in special interest groups with the ability to have their voices heard, it is almost a certainty that large corporations will repeatedly face hostile critics, possibly lots of them. With all those monitoring eyes, to say nothing of Web sites, there is no longer any place on earth to hide. Critics include environmentalists and labor groups, but they also come at you from a host of other directions, including community groups, minorities, patient groups, animal rightists, antigrowth activists, and social conservatives. And don't forget powerful internal pressure groups: your own employees and activist shareholders.

Consider the outcry against Disney as the company was on the

verge of opening its new theme park in September 2005 in Hong
Kong. Groups such as the Sea Shepherd Conservation Society and
the Animals Asia Foundation lobbied hard to prevent Disney from
serving shark's fin soup at the theme park. Although the dish has
been a traditional favorite of the Chinese for generations, served frequently at banquets and weddings, environmentalists pressured the
company to eliminate the soup from its theme park restaurant
menus due to concerns over the diminishing shark population. The
controversy was reported in newspapers across the globe. Finally,
chagrined by the negative publicity, Disney agreed to remove the
dish from its restaurants. Ironically, Disney was also criticized for
not adhering to local customs when it initially refused to allow alco-
hol to be served at Disney Paris. But would Disney have been better
served to have made the decision sooner? Of course it would have.
But making the decision to acquiesce to critics is never easy, especially when you fear it may open you up to even more pressure if you
are perceived as an easy mark.

Sooner or later, most companies are likely to be spotlighted in
the media—whether on television, in blogs, or in traditional print
media—in a way that paints them in a negative light. Apart from embarrassment, and a likely harmful effect on its stock price, negative
stories are increasingly likely to affect purchasing decisions. According to the Natural Marketing Institute, about 63 million Americans,
with a purchasing power of more than $227 billion, pay close atten-
tion to corporate behavior.[8]

Companies are taking notice. Whirlpool, number 18 on a list of
"100 Best Corporate Citizens for 2005" compiled by *Business Ethics*
magazine, believes that "consumers in many cultures choose
Whirlpool among the 'sea of white boxes' because of its commitment
to energy efficiency and pollution control." It has discovered a strong
correlation between a company's performance in appliance markets
and its social response to issues.[9]

Most of the "aware third" of U.S. consumers identified by the
Natural Marketing Institute as being concerned with more than
just a product's price and quality are not activists themselves.[10]
They may not research every product they buy or even look to see

what a company's Web site says about corporate practices. But they'll pay attention to the media and remember negative stories longer than you hope they might. A significant number may also become accustomed to checking out Web sites such as buyblue.org or idealswork.com that detail a company's strategies and behavior. Idealswork.com—whose tagline is "What companies do. What you can do about it"—allows consumers to rank companies based on such issues as executive compensation, retirement plan stability, involvement in weapons manufacturing, and treatment of minorities. Its mission, say founders Sam Pierce and Dan Porter, is to "empower individuals and organizations to align their actions with their values. Our approach is to make social and environmental issues show up on companies' short-term radar."[11]

Although it may be difficult today to link corporate values to consumer purchasing decisions, it is not difficult to envision a time when most customers routinely check for information about a company before making a purchasing decision. The Internet has made this a relatively simple process. This growing need to "buy right" comes from both sides of the political spectrum. While green proponents on the left of the dial are emphasizing environmental and other social concerns, religious-based purchasing is also on the rise, especially in the United States. The American Family Association, for example, a group with a mission to "change the culture to reflect biblical truth," claimed in the fall of 2004 that its 200,000 member group had persuaded Geico, Best Buy, Foot Locker, and others to stop advertising on Comedy Central's *South Park*, which it considers offensive.[12] More recently, it pressured Ford Motor Company into agreeing to stop advertising in gay-themed publications. Then Ford flip-flopped after being sharply criticized by gay and lesbian advocacy groups. So Ford received criticism from both sides before settling on no change of policy.

It is the youngest consumers who will drive this trend to its logical conclusion. They are already accustomed to searching the Web to seek out even the most trivial information, and will have no hesitancy about integrating Web searching into their buying decisions.

You don't need a mass of pressure groups to spark negative

publicity. "It only takes one person with a computer to discover something is wrong with the supply chain and broadcast it all over the world," notes Sandra Waddock, professor of management at the Carroll School of Management, Boston College.[13]

A good example is the problem the Coca-Cola Company experienced in India. An activist, Amit Srivastava, the lone member of a group called Global Resistance, accused the company of "stealing water, poisoning land, and destroying livelihoods all across India." With an annual budget of about $60,000 accumulated through various grants, Srivastava has taken on the giant soft-drink company that had revenues in 2004 of $22 billion. Despite the disparity in size and power, Srivastava has become a central figure in a global campaign by NGOs that has cost Coke millions of dollars in lost sales and legal fees in India and growing damage to its reputation across the globe. In India the campaign has actually shut down bottling plants because of still-unproven claims that they drain and pollute local water supplies. Srivastava's Web site, www.indiaresource.org, also helped pass legislation in India to require soft-drink makers to list pesticide residues on their labels. The Web site, which draws about 20,000 visitors a month, serves as a global platform for local activists and protesters throughout India. Its central complaint is that Coke shouldn't be locating bottling plants in drought-stricken areas. Some of its efforts could be viewed as little more than publicity stunts, but that doesn't dilute their effectiveness. Last year NGOs spread the ridiculous story that Indian farmers were spraying Coke on their crops as a pesticide. "Things grow better with Coke" read a headline in Britain's *Guardian* newspaper.

Srivastava is now spending much of his time rallying U.S. college students to the idea that Coke's "excessive" use of water and pesticides is contributing to pollution and waste disposal problems in India. At least a half-dozen colleges, including Bard in New York, Carleton in Minnesota, and Oberlin in Ohio, have agreed to boycott Coke.

Srivastava grew up in India, but now lives thousands of miles away, in Northern California. His experience is illustrative of how one individual can, via the Web, leverage significant power and cause great harm to a corporation. Or as *The Wall Street Journal* reported, "That a one-man NGO armed with just a laptop computer, a Web site and a telephone calling card can, with his allies, influence a huge multinational corporation illustrates the role social activists can play in a world that's going increasingly online."[14]

Bringing Critics to the Table

In most instances, engaging with critics can achieve common ground. According to the study, by Professor Waddock of Boston College, of more than one hundred multinational corporations in the apparel and footwear sectors, the data showed that the pressures companies are facing from outsiders are often centered on five specific demands:[15]

1. *Integrity:* Stakeholders are demanding that companies be honest; firmly adhere to their stated codes and values; be healthy, whole and financially sound; and in other ways take actions relevant to specific stakeholders. Essentially they expect company rhetoric to match the reality of its actions.
2. *Respect:* Stakeholders are demanding interactive relationships that take into account different points of view when making decisions.
3. *Standards:* Stakeholders are demanding that values be articulated and that at a minimum they adhere to a baseline of internationally agreed values around core issues such as working conditions, human rights, the environment, and integrity.
4. *Transparency:* Stakeholders increasingly demand openness about company performance on the triple bottom line of economic, social, and environmental impacts.
5. *Accountability:* Stakeholders are increasingly demanding that companies acknowledge the impact of their actions and take responsibility for them.

According to Waddock, one of the key elements in deflecting critical attention is for top management to make "a serious commitment to responsible practice and articulated values" and to "ensure that everyone in the organization and its supply chain is aware of that commitment and seeks to meet it."

It is clear that companies today must respond to critics in new ways. Arguing the facts and defending your position with critics almost never works. In fact, you shouldn't even worry—too much—about the validity of criticism. Often the goal is not so much to change minds as it is to spark a dialogue. Strong CEOs get ahead of the curve by responding to external concerns, engaging with their diverse groups of critics, sticking to the facts, and finding commonalities with the majority of their stakeholders. You certainly don't have to cave in to the demands of every critic, but you must understand your constituencies well enough to know how to find the way to enter into a balanced discussion. Most critical is learning how to be responsive, while at the same time fulfilling your financial duties to your shareholders. The story of Lord Browne and BP, along with those of a few other companies in the line of fire, offers some sound ideas about how to strike that balance.

Changing the Paradigm at BP

Big oil has never been known for its environmental concern, at least not until Lord Browne came along. By all rights he should have been a traditional executive, ready to embrace the industry's stance, promoted most vigorously by the Global Climate Coalition (GCC), that global warming is a myth put forth by fringe groups out of touch with both scientific theory and economic realities. After all, Browne grew up in big oil. He is the son of an executive of Anglo-Iranian Oil, the company that later became British Petroleum. Urged by his father to take a job at BP after graduating from Cambridge with a diploma in physics, he was assigned to work in Alaska as a trainee. There he was caught up during the early 1970s in the wrangling between the industry and environmentalists over the Trans-Alaska Pipeline. In essence, each side wanted its argument to prevail in an all-or-nothing proposition: the efficient transportation of oil versus no impact on the environment. At the same time Browne was rising through the ranks of British Petroleum, scientists were beginning to take note that something serious was happening to the earth's atmosphere. In 1990, the United Nations report on climate change predicted a two-degree rise in global temperatures by 2025 and warned of serious consequences. And in 1996, the World Bank and the World Health Organization got the oil industry's attention by calling for a global phase-out of leaded gasoline.[16] This had a significant impact, although the move toward unleaded gasoline was probably driven more by air quality and health concerns than climate change concerns. The following year, six months before the Kyoto protocol was ratified, Browne decided to get a jump on the change in global attitudes even while other companies continued to deny the very existence of climate change.

"These are issues of tremendous complexity," Browne remembers thinking. "Do you want a clean environment, or do you want hydrocarbons? You may see this as a trade-off, but it is a false one. You have to ask if you want both and in the service of gaining both usually comes technology and better ways of doing things."[17]

One of Browne's first seminal actions that began to move the needle was to establish targets for cuts in carbon dioxide emissions at each BP business unit and to back them up with hefty penalties for noncompliance. After a company-wide study of processes, each unit was bound by a formal contract, negotiated personally with Browne, specifying those targets. Each unit's target took into account the differing levels of carbon dioxide that it was likely to produce, with the proviso that the aggregated targets had to reduce company-wide emissions by approximately 0.5 percent per year in order to achieve the goal of a 10 percent reduction by 2010. To give the contracts teeth, any unit that missed its annual target was charged five times the going rate for a ton of CO_2 against its budget, and all the fines were posted on the company's Web site. Browne furthermore pledged to hire employees with strong "environmental ethics and opinions."[18]

The program worked well by creating an internal market for emissions. Business units that were able to reduce emissions quickly by making process adjustments or by purchasing cost-effective pollution controls could sell their "extra" CO_2 allowances to units which couldn't afford the controls or needed more time to bring their emissions into compliance. Browne also made certain that BP was paying attention to "the easy things, including reducing flaring of gas at production and exploration sites, improving the efficiency of turbines, and making sure vapors weren't escaping into the atmosphere."[19]

As a result of these efforts, BP met its goal of reducing carbon dioxide emissions by 10 percent in 2002, a full eight years earlier than its original target date.[20] During the years leading up to the introduction of the "beyond petroleum" concept in 2000, Browne began to meet regularly with environmental groups to get their take on industry practices. He made it clear that he didn't like confrontation, but he also wasn't inclined to wait until everybody agreed with him. "Yes, we do engage," says Browne. "We don't always agree, but you have a dialogue and you explain your position."[21]

At the same time, Browne began to prod the industry to become more responsible environmentally, leading the way on everything from "developing cleaner fuels to disposing of wastewater."[22]

"I don't think we're going to wake up one morning and find everybody trusts corporations," said Browne, but he pledges to listen to his critics, although not necessarily to follow their advice. He pointed out that transparency was the one thing over which he had total control. "Say to people this is what I'm going to do, have a debate, listen, then go ahead," he urged.[23]

Listening to outsiders is obviously important if you are going to gain their trust. But equally important to Browne was the feedback he received from critics within BP itself. Lee Edwards, CEO of BP Solar and one of the people most responsible for rolling out the Beyond Petroleum campaign, explains that "Browne was willing to be unpopular. He wanted to be different and he was willing to reach out to the most aggressive critics. He felt that in tackling such immense problems as climate change, nothing was impossible, given sufficient time and resources. It was a shock to some when Browne stood up on the stage with the likes of Greenpeace, but Browne forced the organization to be more in synch with public opinion and the perspectives of world political leaders. His acts empowered the organization to do things differently. He committed to finding out the facts and then figuring out what BP could do as a business. He was willing to consider the possibilities that there are merits to other points of views."[24]

"See what's on their minds and at least be able to explore the possibilities," Browne suggests. "Maybe something will come of it that neither of us can see."

When Browne initiated an internal e-mail discussion among employees about how BP could respond to concerns about global warming, he was nearly buried in responses. "To the surprise of many in the company, there was considerable support for Browne's outspoken stance on the environment," Edwards remembers. "The responses showed employees worried about global warming. Their children were talking to them about it, and they thought the company ought to get on the front foot about it."[25]

Browne's dialogue with both employees and NGOs was instrumental in shaping many of BP's approaches to environmental issues. These outside concerns, however, never overrode Browne's conviction that he could be responsive to environmental concerns and still meet his obligations to stockholders. He managed to reduce the company's emissions in a way that actually saved money and increased profits.

Some environmentalists criticize BP's approach of reducing emissions by trading internal emissions because it allows companies to take credit for what could be a very uneven compliance record among business units. Critics are also concerned that, with no good way of monitoring emissions, companies will be tempted to overreport emissions decreases. Yet market-oriented programs like these

are considered by most economists to be "the most cost-effective—
and therefore the most viable—method of cutting down on greenhouse gases."[26]

Companies that decide to engage with critics have to be absolutely certain how far they are willing to go in meeting the desires
of their critics. Establishing a policy and being consistent in implementing it is as essential in this arena as it is with any other business
strategy. That is, the promises made by image advertising should always match what the company is capable of and *willing* to do, not
what it *aspires* to do. BP essentially said to its green constituencies,
"This is all we can do now; we're trying," and then it created a rebranding campaign to get that message across.

Beyond Petroleum

Beyond Petroleum as a rebranding strategy was a direct outgrowth of Browne's conversations with critics and employees.
Launched in 2000, the tagline meant two things to Browne. "In the
first place, it recognized that petroleum would be used for many
years, but that we have to think differently. We have to ask, 'Can we
take the carbon out of it? Can we produce fuels for cars that produce
less CO_2? Can we reduce the amount of emissions BP makes in its
day-to-day operations?' And in the second place, beyond that, we are
investing in alternative energies." The campaign signaled to the
world that BP had its sights on being something other than a major
source of pollution and that it was trying to do its part in solving
very real problems that the company would not be sweeping under
the rug.

But Browne and his team knew they couldn't paint the company
as completely clean and green. Nobody would believe it. "It's a start,"
every element in the corporate ad campaign declared in an appeal to
consumers who wanted their oil company to be part of the solution
rather than the problem. The campaign was intended to reinforce
the notion that beyond this scary thing (pollution), there is a good
thing (an oil company committed to a cleaner environment).

Complicating matters, however, was that at almost the same time the original Beyond Petroleum campaign rolled out, BP began lobbying hard for the opening of the Arctic National Wildlife Refuge (ANWR) to drilling. Browne made it clear that if the 19-million-acre preserve was made available for oil exploration by the U.S. government, BP would consider participating. BP believed that with new, more environmentally sensitive equipment that promised a smaller footprint and little impact on wildlife, the company could safely drill without harming the region. But to many environmentalists, who adamantly argued that too little oil could be extracted to justify the potential damage to the environment, the drive to drill in ANWR was a symbol of the oil industry's disregard for the environment. Environmental groups specifically objected to BP's membership in Arctic Power, a group lobbying for drilling in ANWR. As a result, in 2000 Greenpeace gave Browne an award for "Best Impression of an Environmentalist." Yet, gradually, Browne has won over many environmentalists as BP unabashedly pursues certain environmental positions without giving up its point of view and while pursuing the responsible actions necessary to compete and grow its business.

Since its first introduction of the Beyond Petroleum campaign, BP has been working toward becoming an industry leader in exploring wind power, solar energy, and other power generation technologies, which emit less carbon dioxide. It has stepped up its production of natural gas, which, when used to generate electricity, emits far less carbon dioxide than other fossil fuels, such as coal. BP has also invested in an experimental program in Algeria to pump carbon dioxide produced by its natural gas production project there back into reservoirs far beneath the ground. This "sequestration project" is now depositing about a million tons of CO_2 a year about a mile beneath the sand. If a similar "carbon capture and storage" approach were widely adopted it could be revolutionary, preventing many millions of tons of greenhouse gases from ever being vented into the atmosphere. BP and Ford have pledged $20 million to Princeton University to study how the issue of rising greenhouse gas emissions can be addressed, and even ExxonMobil, a vigorous debunker of global warming in the past, sees the value of such a solution and has promised \$100 million to Stanford University to study the best ways to capture and store CO_2.[27]

BP's evolution into a company that is "beyond petroleum," implying a cause greater than just pulling oil out of the ground, has resonated with a public that expects corporations to act responsibly but has become accustomed to being disappointed. In a series of moves that have seriously quieted its critics, BP has put its efforts where its mouth is. It has become a global leader in removing lead and other pollutants from gasoline, and is now one of the world's leading providers of solar power, with a growth rate of its BP Solar unit of about 30 percent annually.[28] BP has invested in solar for about twenty-five years, but 2004 was the first year the unit turned a profit. Browne also demonstrated his willingness to break from the rest of the oil industry when the company resigned its membership in both the Global Climate Coalition and Arctic Power.

According to Lee Edwards, "Political and economic factors are drivers of growth. On the political side, compliance with the Kyoto treaty, the fact that 'green' is part of the national agenda in many countries, and the reality that energy independence is today linked to security issues, all contribute to greater interest in alternative energy sources. This, coupled with the rising price of conventional sources, is fostering a growing market. Currently Japan and Germany account for about two-thirds of the market, but Spain, California, Korea, and China are emerging. Investment in solar will be stepped up, and we expect to see a profit."

A new phase in BP's corporate reputation campaign, launched in 2005, focuses on the company's commitment to cleaner energy. The home page of its Web site announces that "it's time to start a low-carbon diet" and urges visitors to click for more information about what BP is doing about climate change and about how their own lifestyle choices affect carbon emissions.[29]

In an era of high energy prices, when public and political leaders are scrutinizing top management of energy companies, BP's "green" position differentiates it and sets its management apart. "All things being equal, people prefer to buy environmentally friendly products," says Browne. "But you have to be prepared for things to go wrong. There are no easy answers, so you have to stick to what you believe in, realizing that results in business are often long-term. If you have a problem, an accident, you can hope that people will listen and trust you. But your reputation is not infinite. It will only take you so far. It will help you to manage in difficult times, but you have to do the right thing."[30]

Gaining Power from Critics

In my experience working with clients, I have found that most executives have the same initial reaction to criticism: Let's ignore the interference and see if it will go away. The denial-bad-press-lawsuits-more-bad-press-capitulation model is by far the least effective way of dealing with critics, although it is probably the most common. It's common because as a strategy it may, in fact, have worked for some in the past. Before cyberspace, most oppositional groups could only mount limited campaigns. If a company wished to stonewall and then find itself fighting litigation, it could hope to wear critics out. That may be one reason it took the tobacco companies so long to admit that their products could cause harm. Today, the Phillip Morris Web site states that "Philip Morris USA agrees with the overwhelming medical and scientific consensus that cigarette smoking causes lung cancer, heart disease, emphysema and other serious diseases in smokers. Smokers are far more likely to develop serious diseases, like lung cancer, than non-smokers. There is no safe cigarette."[31] Imagine what the tobacco company chieftains of old would think. But a new day has dawned. Now it is the embracers, not the deniers, who will enjoy the benefits of public confidence.

Of course, no company can afford to abjectly capitulate to every complainer who comes along. A company perceived as an easy mark would soon drown in frivolous lawsuits. The executive who wants his company or division to deal effectively with critics will prepare a suite of responses, appropriate to the situation. This is not crisis management; in fact, it is the opposite. Think of it as a new kind of opportunity management.

Threat Level and Newsworthiness

If we think about responses to criticism analytically, we understand that the difficulties created by critics arise on two significant dimensions: threat level and newsworthiness. Threats range from revelations that could destroy a company's reputation or put it into bankruptcy to those that no one would be bothered by even if they received intense attention. In the newsworthiness category, companies must measure what Deutsche Bank analyst Bill Dreher calls "headline risk."[32] How bad for business would it be if people were to read about your critics' charges over their morning coffee? Would it be any worse for your company if they continued to read about them regularly over the course of days, weeks, months, or years? What if Web sites and blogs were devoted to these issues? Newsworthiness is also a measure of how much people care. If your critics evoke only a shrug from your customers and other stakeholders, newsworthiness will be less of a factor in your decision. And if your stakeholders aren't the ones complaining—if the criticism is coming from true outsiders with no impact on your company's future but with simply an ax to grind—the threat level is also reduced. But how many true outsiders are there in today's instant-communications world? Not many. It is best to be ready to respond to any critic and to match the vigor of your response to the threat and newsworthiness levels posed.

There are at least three factors to consider when weighing the threat and newsworthiness of any situation:

Preempting Criticism. The best kind of criticism is no criticism at all, but when criticism is inevitable, an early, jujitsu-like response is preferable. In fact, you can take the power from critics by making your own principled response to brewing problems. Lord Browne earned himself a lot of breathing room simply by saying, "You're right. Let's solve this." Added to that was BP's decision to show its commitment to action by changing its business practices in ways suggested by its critics. If emissions were the main problem in global warming, that was where BP would concentrate its response. Its actions have earned it favorable notice, particularly among the segment of the buying public that is environmentally aware but not activist. That's because BP is seen as at least *trying* to deal reasonably with complex issues. Its critics, therefore, have consistently remained on the low ends of the chart in both threat and newsworthiness.

Refute and Redirect. Often the criticism will seem unjust. It may even conflict with your business model. That doesn't mean you must change your strategy. In the case of Wal-Mart, for example, the newsworthiness of its struggles to keep out union workers, to review pensions and health-care costs, keep labor costs low, and to outcompete mom-and-pop stores has been high. But the company has long perceived the threat level of such criticism to be low. CEO Lee Scott considers many of his critics to be people who wouldn't shop at his stores even if they all became unionized, started paying higher wages, and propped up independent competitors. His critics, he told *The Economist*, are "found among the small group of people who . . . exist in every country and who distrust institutions and do not like big business." Where Wal-Mart has slipped up, according to Scott, is in allowing such critics to trigger complaints and lawsuits that allege the company is "nasty."[33]

In the past, Scott has gone so far as to blame the company's falling reputation (it no longer tops *Fortune*'s Most Admired Companies list) on greedy unions.[34] But even Scott sees that times have changed and that the way to address critics is to listen to them, to change the dialogue to what Wal-Mart is doing well rather than what Wal-Mart is doing badly. Toward that end, the company has begun to post on its Web site detailed data on its wages, health-care plans, charitable giving, and impact on the economy,[35] and it has opened itself up to the idea of expanding its health-care coverage to part-time workers. It has also begun partnering with environmental groups to purchase threatened wilderness areas, including one of the largest stands of old-growth ponderosa pine left in the world.[36] Even if Scott's original contention was correct and Wal-Mart is responding to a threat that may not be important to most of its customers, he clearly sees a larger threat from people not feeling good about shopping in his stores. He is wise to be concerned. A *New York Times* story reporting on an internal Wal-Mart memo that suggested ways to cut employee benefit costs was one of the most viewed business news articles on nytimes.com in all of 2005.[37]

Delay and Adjust. What do you do when critics might have a point, but your business model makes it impossible—at least at first blush—to do anything effective to correct the problem? Nike found itself in just this situation when critics pounced on it after a 1992 *Harper's Magazine* story showcased "appalling working conditions" at Nike's overseas factories.[38] Those conditions weren't very different from those in factories run by Nike's competitors in low-wage countries, but it was Nike that felt the brunt of words and pictures in publications across the globe. Organizations like the Clean Clothes Campaign, a European coalition of NGOs and trade unions,[39] publicized the company's practices and urged consumers to shun Nike sneakers.

Company officials at first responded defensively, arguing lamely that its plants were at least as good as those of its competitors. That only served to make the critics noisier, especially when Nike refused to make public the locations of its manufacturers.[40] On the threat-newsworthiness scale, Nike was creating a significant problem for itself. Newsworthiness was enhanced with stories of people suffering, and the threat increased as activists sensed that Nike was vulnerable to a boycott of its products.

Early in the confrontation, Nike hired a group of high-profile personalities like former ambassador to the United Nations Andrew Young to audit its labor practices. Their conclusion that "all was well" in the supply chain changed no one's mind. Finally Nike decided it could no longer afford to let the damage to its reputation continue. It established labor codes for compensation and treatment of workers to which all its suppliers were expected to adhere. That did little to solve the problem, however, because it turned out that Nike's supply-chain model actually rewarded suppliers who treated their workers badly by basing performance incentives on price, quality, and delivery times. No wonder suppliers were slow to adhere to Nike's new code of conduct. Founder and chairman Phil Knight spent the last years of his tenure as CEO remaking Nike's business model so that suppliers are instead graded on their compliance with the company's labor code. Nike procurement teams are now rewarded or "taxed" on the quality of the suppliers they use, while still being rewarded for financial and quality performance.[41] And in April 2005 Nike made the locations of all of its seven hundred suppliers public.[42] It also posts on its Web site reports of problems in its manufacturing operations, including child-labor violations and the regions where they occurred. The company is the first in its industry to be transparent about its supply chain. It is a tough balancing act, but Nike's efforts have earned it praise and quieted its critics.

Learn from Past Experience. Banks don't typically become the target of environmental activists, so Citigroup could be excused for being unprepared for controversy when it received a seemingly harmless letter asking it to stop making loans on projects that would destroy rain forests. Both threat and newsworthiness levels were quite low at this point, even after members of the Rainforest Action Network (RAN) organized protest rallies and an internet campaign urging customers to cut up their Citigroup credit cards. Only twenty thousand customers complied, so no one in the news media paid much attention, and neither did Citibank. But RAN gradually turned up the heat, and suddenly activists were hanging a massive

banner on the side of Citigroup's Manhattan headquarters that
played on the bank's own slogan. "FOREST DESTRUCTION & GLOBAL
WARMING?" it read. "WE'RE BANKING ON IT." RAN volunteers later
chained themselves to the doors of bank branches, picketed speeches
by then chairman Sanford Weill, and ran ads featuring celebrities
destroying their Citibank cards. As the newsworthiness level rose, so
did the threat level, much to the dismay of Citigroup, which was
loath to have stakeholders believe that they were in some way contributing to the destruction of old-growth forests. Four years into
the escalation, Citigroup agreed to negotiate with RAN, and finally
to promise not to loan money to "projects that degrade critical natural habitats."[43]

In hindsight, an objective observer of the threat-newsworthiness
scale might have concluded that Citibank should have negotiated
long before the company's risk level grew. But being the first bank to
be theatrically attacked for the environmental impacts of its loans
seems to have made Weill believe that the protesters would tire of
their tactics before Citigroup did. He was wrong, as were others in
the banking industry who took notice and changed their assessment
of both the threat and newsworthiness of this sort of behavior once
they were drawn into the protests. In 2005 activists in environmental
protective suits protested on the sidewalks of Chicago and New York
JP Morgan Chase's alleged financing of illegal logging in Indonesia
and human rights violations at a mine in Peru. Just two weeks later
the bank announced a change in its lending policies in order to prevent any such abuses in the future.[44] It benefited from Citigroup's experience and had time to internalize the notion that in today's
business world well-funded and experienced NGOs know how to
keep raising the stakes. As a result, the threat of an ongoing business
disruption was quickly realized and eliminated.

Bringing Critics Inside

As difficult as it may be for some executives to admit, immediate negotiation is the best response when facing a well-established,

media-savvy critic. Study the problem and determine the facts for yourself so that you can clarify your position. Evaluate whether this is a problem likely to capture the attention of a significant number of customers, employees, or other stakeholders who believe that your company should take action. Perform due diligence on every critic and decide how much each can potentially escalate your threat-newsworthiness equation. Then do what you know is right, which will help you preserve or enhance your company's reputation and further your leadership position over the long term. Critics with substantial resources and proven records of attracting media attention should be considered important stakeholders and brought to the table.

Many companies have trouble taking critics seriously, whether they are activist groups, customers, or even shareholders or competitors. That is a mistake. A persistent barrage of criticism can do more damage in a shorter amount of time than almost any other challenge. Resilient executives have accepted that, in this business environment, their actions will always be under a microscope. They recognize that allowing critics to offer constructive feedback generates valuable goodwill. Often, merely listening to negative feedback is a powerful way to defuse criticism before it becomes destructive. Engaging with critics—before your competitors do—can also be a competitive tool, as illustrated by companies like BP. But beyond that, strong leaders accept the idea that sometimes a critic will have a good idea that will make a company better.

Today, instant global communication gives every pressure group the potential to amplify its voice many times over. That gives them the power to lower your revenues, increase your costs, and damage your company's reputation. Even if critics are not at your door today, they could be there tomorrow. Most companies are taken completely by surprise when criticism surfaces. Instead, corporate leaders want to defuse criticism, sometimes before it even begins. Ideally, you want to get inside critics' heads and change the terms of the interaction. You want to hear the distant sounds of potential discontent and pay sufficient attention to the possible long-term consequences. Only in that way can you get ahead of your critics and correct potential threats to your profits and reputation before they do any damage.

As a leader, you must demand regular updates from responsible employees on what's being whispered about your company. Once an attack appears in the mainstream media or in a lawsuit, it's too late; your reputation will have already begun to suffer. According to editor Ronald J. Alsop, of *The Wall Street Journal*, smart companies "are trolling chat rooms, discussion boards, online news media and Web sites run by their competitors and critics to detect rumblings that could end up making headlines if a reporter or financial analyst discovers them first. Companies should think of a Web-based threat to their reputation as a particularly dangerous virus that can spread to infect millions of people in a matter of hours or even minutes."[45]

Internal systems specifically designed to monitor the buzz about your company can help to discover trouble early and enable you to take immediate action by personally approaching your critics. It's very unlikely any of them will turn down a chance to meet with you. Just reaching out a hand in peace ratchets the hostility level down a bit. Even if you are not the CEO, you can open a dialogue with critics who are calling on your company to change its practices or philosophy of doing business.

Build a bridge that allows dialogue. If you can't make the immediate changes your critics are demanding—and you usually can't—you can at least get credit for expressing regret for some of your company's past actions based on policies that have since been changed. Yes, the lawyers will say never apologize or you'll open yourself up to lawsuits. But carefully done, without admitting actionable specifics, these expressions of regret can definitely lower the tension level. They also just might be good business. Studies of medical malpractice have shown that injured parties either don't sue or settle for less when an apology is forthcoming.[46] Even if you don't think you have anything to apologize for, you'll want to acknowledge that your critics have concerns they feel are legitimate.

You can almost always find some common ground with your critics. Identify at least one specific issue you can agree to work toward and make that the centerpiece of your efforts. For Lord Browne, striving toward the goal of a 10 percent emissions reduction, calmed his most vocal critics, particularly after BP met and then exceeded its self-imposed deadlines. This is when you can establish enough trust to encourage a free exchange of views. Employees should be instructed not to criticize the critics the company is working with, and executives must free up sufficient time to constructively hear their concerns.

Once you make changes in response to criticism, make sure word gets out. Act jointly with your critics in announcing new programs or directions. Your goal is to turn the criticism into positive feelings about your company, enough positive feelings to diminish the credibility of critical attacks.

Checklist for Dialoguing with Critics

1. **Pay attention to small voices.** Be aware that information moves around the world at a more rapid pace than ever before in history. Economies appear more volatile than ever, and there are no corners of the world so remote that your footprint can remain hidden. A small voice of criticism in a tiny market can quickly magnify to reach your most important stakeholders.

2. **Prepare for things to go wrong and accept that criticism is a fact of life.** There are no formulas for avoiding critics. It is safe to assume that at some point in time your company will be in a negative spotlight with unfavorable publicity.

3. **Adopt a culture of being open to other points of view.** Train employees to listen to those with opposing views. You often inherit a way of looking at the world, but be willing to set that aside and look at the world in a new way.

4. **Commit to a regular exchange with critics.** Institute processes and assign responsibilities to insure that there is dialogue and outreach to third parties.

5. **Be honest about what you can do, and then do it.** Listen to the views of critics, but be honest about what you are and are not willing to do. Never be seduced by the desire to please, and don't commit to what is not reasonably possible.

6. **Realize that there is no easy answer.** Many NGOs live by their mission and the visibility they gain with their protests. Sometimes no solution will be possible. The goal is to establish a dialogue, based on trust, that lessens tension and enables both sides to listen and understand.

6

Courageous Realism Conquers Wishful Thinking

Men willingly believe what they wish.

Julius Caesar,
Commentaries on the Gallic War

*It's important for CEOs to look at themselves in the
mirror and really look, as opposed to using external
audiences as their mirrors.*

Fred Hassan,
CEO and Chairman,
Schering-Plough Corporation[1]

WHEN A COMPANY suffers a sudden financial collapse after years
of profitability, it typically comes as a shock to shareholders, customers, and employees. It is not, however, a surprise to everyone. A
dramatic reversal of fortune is usually the result of years of mistakes, lack of attention, and poor business decisions. Most likely,
there are employees in the ranks who have known all along that all
is not well. They may even have been sending warnings up the chain
of command, frantically signaling that trouble lies ahead. Often
such reports are dismissed as irrelevant, or the employee is intimi-
dated into silence by management's adherence to forecasts about

the rosy long-term prospects of the company. Remarkably, the company's misjudgments can be obvious to everyone except top management, who can often be the last to admit that serious problems exist. "Don't those people at the top see what's happening?" employees wonder.

Unfortunately, in many cases, the answer is "No, they don't." The reason they don't is that they have a serious, often fatal, case of wishful thinking, the opposite of hard-nosed realism. "We are creative narrators of stories that tend to allow us to do what we want and justify what we have done," asserts Ann Tenbrunsel, codirector of the Institute for Ethical Business Worldwide at Notre Dame University. "We believe our stories and thus believe that we are objective about ourselves. It's kind of dismal how hard it is to change the stories that get told in companies."[2]

Take the example of Carly Fiorina, the highly visible, charismatic head of Hewlett-Packard. Fiorina was HP's first CEO to be selected from the outside, and she assumed her role with the intention of transforming the company. Her drive to shake things up was most evident in HP's controversial acquisition of Compaq. Morale at the company sank to all time lows when Fiorina implemented the largest downsizing in HP's history. But Fiorina continued to be bullish, underscoring her confidence that the greater scale achieved by the merger would provide the competitive edge necessary to enhance performance. But as HP's share price dropped, so, too, did the board's confidence in Fiorina. She never saw it coming. Only a few days before the HP board announced her departure, Fiorina told reporters at the World Economic Forum that her relationship with the board was "excellent."[3]

The importance of facing reality may seem self-evident, but it can be surprisingly difficult to practice when a company starts to slip and begins to disappoint its shareholders. Fiorina never acknowledged to herself that her bullish, forceful ways, with power centered in her office, were increasingly at odds with the board's perspective on the best way to lead the company. In denial of the impact of lagging share performance, internal morale issues, and departures of top talent, Fiorina lost her footing and was toppled from her position as head of HP.

It's not a matter of not knowing; it's a matter of ignoring what you know and framing weaknesses in a favorable light even in the face of what a dose of realism would recognize as difficult times ahead. Executives and board members who are caught up in wishful thinking are often unable to see past their own psychological biases, biases that have been strengthened over the years by constant exposure to the company's positive stories. These stories are particularly persuasive and can become legendary when the company's underlying results are strong. It is only when these stories begin to diverge from reality that they cause trouble. The very human tendency to want to continue to believe, to see our companies and ourselves in the most favorable possible light, can lead to disaster.

Wishful Thinking Run Amok

Wishful thinking has been the downfall of dozens of companies in recent years. Take the case of Richard Jay Kogan, who had been an executive with the pharmaceutical company Schering-Plough for sixteen years when he took over as chairman and CEO in September 1998. The following year the company celebrated its fourteenth straight year of dividend increases and earnings growth. Any realistic observer, however, could have known the company was poised for a downturn.

One of Schering-Plough's biggest problems arose from the fact that its blockbuster product, the "nondrowsy" prescription allergy drug Claritin, was due to lose its patent protection in 2002. With sales of $3.2 billion in 2001, Claritin was contributing a third of the company's total sales and 40 percent of its profits.[4] Management was banking on successful reformulation of Claritin, to be introduced to the market as Clarinex, to protect the brand from patent expiration, ignoring a more realistic outlook that would have led to a different conclusion: Branded drug products' sales and profits *always* significantly decline when patents run out. Making matters worse for

Schering-Plough, Roche Pharmaceuticals was about to launch a competing hepatitis drug that in only a year's time would grab a large share of the hepatitis market, another of the Schering's key franchises.[5] Yet the company continued to insist that all was well and that its drug pipeline contained numerous promising drugs that would compensate for the loss of sales.[6]

Kogan and his management team did not move to realistically address issues which were springing up in various parts of the organization. Wishful thinking led them to ignore the warning signs of fundamental weaknesses throughout the company, in the developmental pipeline, and in the performance of many of the company's most important products. It led to a lack of discipline by an unfocused leadership that refused to confront problems.

Kogan knew that Claritin's primary patent protection would expire in 2002, yet when he took over in September 1998 he insisted that "Schering-Plough's major businesses are performing well and achieving solid results. Assuming no unforeseen developments, Schering-Plough expects to turn in another good year of earnings growth in 1998, with earnings per share expected to be higher by about 20 percent." He also turned aside suggestions that the company would need to merge with another pharmaceutical company to survive, and in an interview with *The Wall Street Journal* he neglected to mention that Schering-Plough was under government investigation.[7] In June of the following year management was still denying weaknesses and rejecting calls for a merger, citing "strong growth prospects" based on several add-on patents for Claritin and a strong pipeline containing numerous drugs in development for the treatment of cancer and other diseases.[8]

In his dealings with the financial press, Kogan was also taking a head-in-the-sand approach to other problems. Since at least 1998, the company had been under government investigation for selling its drugs to private health-care providers at prices lower than it sold them to Medicaid, a violation of federal law."[9] The FDA was also investigating claims that Schering-Plough had for years failed to manufacture its products safely at plants in New Jersey and Puerto

Rico.[10] Yet Kogan still boldly predicted in public statements that "2001 will be seen as a watershed year, when this company undertook important changes to remake itself."[11] When questioned, Kogan declined to say whether or not the FDA was widening its probe of safety violations, or whether other products might be delayed.[12]

As all of this was happening, management continued to report strong quarterly numbers. They built optimism and hoped that future revenue would remain stable even amid mounting problems. Such behavior is not all that unusual in corporate America. There is nothing atypical in management reporting strong quarterly numbers without warning that tough times are ahead. No one wants to spoil a party with an announcement that brush fires are beginning to ignite in different parts of the forest. But hope, without a plan for success, is just wishful thinking.

Kogan's response was to withdraw further from talking to the media and the investment community, for the most part even ceasing to participate in the company's quarterly conference calls with analysts. He disappeared into his office, with most employees knowing him only from his annual chairman's letter.

But Kogan's disappearance couldn't hide the continuing bad news. Claritin lost its patent protection, taking with it more than $1 billion in sales. The add-on drug, Clarinex, intended to preserve patent-level pricing, was delayed for more than a year because of the company's failure to comply with manufacturing regulations. The FDA slapped the company with a consent decree requiring it to pay a fine of $500 million and forcing it to suspend the manufacture of 73 drugs and improve production processes for another 120. The result was a loss of roughly $300 million in sales and another $100 million in costs to comply with FDA standards.

Finally, in early 2002, as Schering-Plough's stock price was plunging, Kogan belatedly recognized the need to paint a more realistic picture for investors. Ironically, the first announcement only served to exacerbate the company's problems further—not because Kogan was finally becoming more forthright in his public disclosure of Schering-Plough's problems,[13] but because he initially confided in

only a select group of analysts, telling them that the company's true
financial outlook was in fact dismal. The SEC promptly accused
Schering-Plough of improperly divulging critical financial information by not releasing it to all investors simultaneously. Although he
admitted no wrongdoing, Kogan himself paid $50,000 in penalties
and stepped down from his job shortly thereafter. The company ultimately agreed to pay a $1 million fine to settle the case.[14]

Promises That Cannot be Kept

Schering-Plough is, of course, not the only company that has
suffered the consequences of wishful thinking. Far from it. It is an
ailment that can afflict us all because it is human nature to remain
optimistic in the face of setbacks. But optimism is only helpful when
combined with a pragmatic, realistic plan for success.

Take a look, for example, at Qwest Communications, which at
the beginning of this decade seemed poised to become a top communications company. According to allegations in a civil action by
the SEC, in mid-2000 when Qwest purchased US West, then CEO
Joe Nacchio promised 20 percent annual earnings growth by 2005.
During investor conference calls in early 2001, he confirmed the positive outlook, stating that the company expected 12 percent revenue
growth in the first quarter compared to the same period in 2000,
which was "two to three times the rate of everyone in the industry,"
the SEC said.[15]

These projections represented a classic case of wishful thinking.
Nacchio and other top executives fostered a corporate culture in
which meeting short-term targets became a mantra. Anyone who
didn't agree with the tactics he used to make his numbers was considered "not part of the team."[16]

Even after the company drew down its entire $4 billion emer-
gency bank line to meet its cash needs, Nacchio continued to deny
there were problems, telling investors in a conference call "Liquidity
is not an issue for Qwest."[17] Employees were instructed to toe the
line and commit to the story of strong, profitable growth, regardless

of the facts. According to a civil suit filed by the Securities and Exchange Commission, Nacchio had created "a culture of fear" during
his tenure as CEO of Qwest so severe that employees willingly became complicit in misleading investors about the company's financial condition.[18]

Finally, as the company's stock was plummeting from a high of
$64 a share on its way to a low of $1.20, Nacchio was fired by the
board of directors. Afterward, former executive Nik Nesbitt told *Fortune*: "It became an 'I just gotta do what the boss says' company."[19]
Wishful thinking had become a corporate value.

Restoring the Power of Trust

The seeds of wishful thinking are relatively easy to spot. Much
more difficult is a new CEO's job of reversing years of the behavior. At
Qwest, Richard Notebaert, who the board of directors brought in to replace Nacchio, scrambled to save the company from the brink by looking for acquisitions that would immediately boost sales and profits. But
more important, he dictated an end to overpromising. The company, he
declared, would now have to live by the "newspaper test," in that nothing would be done that anyone in the company wouldn't want to see on
a newspaper's front page.[20] The company essentially broke even in
2005, if onetime write-offs are discounted, but Notebaert is still not
overpromising. "We have an opportunity to cross over to profitability in
2006," he told analysts. "It's pretty plausible that it will happen."[21]

At Schering-Plough, Fred Hassan, who in April 2003 was named
CEO and chairman, had an equally daunting task. Hassan had a reputation as a builder of companies, as a skilled leader who could fix
troubled operations, and as a person of integrity. At his previous job
as CEO of Pharmacia, he had increased revenues by $5.1 billion and
tripled earnings per share two years after the difficult merger of the
Swedish company Pharmacia and Upjohn. Yet despite Hassan's impressive record, he had his work cut out for him if he was going to
save Schering-Plough from bankruptcy. The year he took over from
Kogan, the company lost $92 million after an 18 percent drop in

revenue, and it was still facing fines totaling more than a $1 billion, a staggering sum. No wonder the company had lost two-thirds of its market value in less than three years.

Schering-Plough–Fred Hassan Named Chairman and CEO in April 2003

Four-year monthly stock performance for Schering-Plough

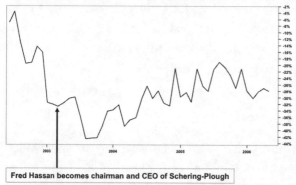

Fred Hassan becomes chairman and CEO of Schering-Plough

To the credit of Schering-Plough's board, once the full picture of the company's issues had been brought to its attention, it knew it needed to go outside the company for a change agent willing to take drastic steps to turn things around. But even Hassan was surprised at what he found his first day on the job. "The company was in much worse shape than I expected," says Hassan,[22] recalling that the lack of controls was so profound that no one could even tell him which products were making money and which weren't. But he recognized that Schering-Plough's problems went well beyond expiring patents, lackluster new products, and regulatory scrutiny. These were only the symptoms; the disease was a much more fundamental abandonment of the power of trust—trust in Schering-Plough's ability to rebound from its problems, trust in the need for the company's employees to hear some straight talk if they were to be part of the solution.

Hassan understood that his first priority had to be to restore confidence among each of the company's stakeholders, beginning with his own employees. He needed to implement new priorities at the company, which he articulated in a new corporate theme, "Strive to earn trust every day." He communicated this directly to employees, urging them to stay in tune with stakeholders. He understood that it had become difficult for people to feel good about coming to work every day, and he set out to change that. He promoted a "new way of working," in which hard work and realistic forecasts would truly, as he said, "build a new Schering-Plough into a new kind of healthcare company—one that earns trust, and delivers high performance for the long term."[23]

To illustrate his commitment to keeping employees informed about the status of their company and engage them in the rebuilding process, Hassan began a series of unusually frank town hall meetings. The first was held three days after he was named CEO. He outlined a five-stage action agenda, with stabilization the immediate requirement leading to repair, turnaround, breakout, and, finally, long-term strength. By then the first step, communicating the extent of the company's weaknesses, with full disclosure no matter what the fallout, was already under way.

Hassan also made it a top priority to articulate an equally clear statement of the condition of the company to stockholders. During his first conference call with analysts, he didn't pull punches. A survey by Thompson First Call revealed that analysts had expected Hassan to announce a 28 percent increase in earnings. Instead, he told them, bold measures were going to be necessary to save the company, and before any turnaround he expected profits to plunge 67 percent in 2003 and fall again the following year.

After that bombshell, Hassan felt it was important to return to solid footing as quickly as possible. He announced a plan to cut costs by $200 million, which included freezing salaries and suspending profit-sharing payments for the first time in forty-seven years. Hassan says he "tried to educate people on the facts," but that the toughest decision he made, which shocked the financial community, was the dividend cut. It was the first time a large pharmaceutical company had ever cut its dividend, but Hassan felt it was necessary to make a dramatic statement that business as usual was no longer acceptable. Hassan took some personal criticism for the tough medicine, but his candid comments and forceful actions set a new tone.

At the same time Hassan was cutting these costs, he was increasing the R&D budget to $1.5 billion in an effort to explore new compounds and molecular targets and build a new drug pipeline with innovative products. Hassan also maximized the company's investment by trying to fill about half the pipeline with treatments obtained via licensing and partnerships.

Hassan knew that stringent measures were needed to give everyone in the company a new way of seeing that things were going to get better and not return to the unrealistic mind-set of the previous era. To accomplish this, he would need to continue to promote an open evaluation of the company's strengths and weaknesses and sustain his commitment to ongoing communications with all key stakeholders. He began making regular, personal contacts with employees at all levels, particularly among what he calls "the frontline people, and the people who manage the frontline people." He also reached out to the places where the information on which to base good decisions could reliably be found. Hassan understood that a stockpile of goodwill can be built by simply making the effort to be attentive and visible, that little things like answering your e-mails can go a long way toward earning the trust of your employees. Hassan even closed the formal executive dining room in order "to set the right tone."[24]

Still, Hassan knew that these measures were not nearly enough to reestablish Schering-Plough as a competitive company. He had to attract new people and build new processes. As a guide for employees, he instituted a set of six standard leadership behaviors to help convey the values he intended to impress on the new Schering-Plough:

1. Shared accountability and transparency
2. Cross-functional teamwork and collaboration
3. Listening and learning, open-minded behaviors
4. Benchmarking and continuous improvement
5. Coaching and developing others
6. Business integrity

Hassan understood the importance of the power of a confident workforce, especially in the face of significant staff reductions. He moved quickly to create an "action agenda, a framework that would allow people to see how things would work in the future." He focused on assuring people that they were valued, and believed that "if we stay focused and have faith in ourselves and do the right things, we could come out of the darkness."[25]

"In these circumstances," Hassan recalls, "it was extremely important for people to have a sense of self-confidence and self-worth, and I tried my best to reach out and get people to feel that way. It was important to go through a listen-and-learn process, then move forward to lead us out of the tough spot we were in."[26] Hassan wanted to completely alter expectations by creating an environment that would allow people to accomplish their goals by removing hurdles, thus "creating a motivational environment so that they want to do what needs to get done."[27]

From his experience during the turnaround at Pharmacia, Hassan knew he would need to establish new performance expectations and metrics for realistically measuring employee performance. There would be no more wishful thinking that performance would improve by saying it would, or that a few changes would make a difference. No more hiding from reality. As he had done at Pharmacia, Hassan reached out to top managers personally—not just by organization-chart dotted lines, but by how much they contributed to achieving the company's goals—even if they were junior employees. Hassan felt he needed, above all, to establish an in-company network that would keep him informed about what was really happening on the ground. He needed to be fully informed in order to engage in the type of rebuilding that would put the company on a solid footing.

Linking Strategy with Execution

Hassan called another company-wide town hall meeting in April 2005 to celebrate the progress that had been made. He spent the better part of the meeting talking about the tools that had been put into place using the company's new "core document" that would guide the new Schering-Plough. According to the document, the senior management team would move from a review committee to an operational team. The composition of the committee was also altered to include the head of R&D, which Hassan felt would be the main driver of long-term value creation. A highly regarded head of quality was also added to the team, as was a new person in charge of compliance and business integrity to report directly to the CEO. The chief financial officer—another new hire—was now expected to be more of a business partner who would be responsible for financial forecasting. Other fresh faces at the top of what Hassan was building into a truly globalized enterprise included new heads of the prescription pharmaceutical business, global manufacturing and supply, and human resources. Hassan stressed that the team would be a much more open group, with stronger convergence and shared information, all focused on common goals.

A key component of the core document, according to Hassan, were the six "leader behaviors," cited above, specific standards that all company leaders must live up to. "Behavior is important because the business culture is a result of not just ideas or speeches, but of actions," Hassan says. "We believe that the right attitude drives the right behaviors. By converging around very specific behaviors, we are making the right actions happen."[28]

Another key piece of Hassan's concept of managing the new Schering-Plough is "situational leadership," meaning simply that decisions should be made according to the situation, according to whether it was urgent or routine. Some decisions will be made at the top by the CEO or other top executive, but there are also many decisions that should be made by whoever is in the best position to know the right thing to do. Hassan believes that appropriate decisions can be made in both these zones, but that most situations call for "participative" decision making in which leaders and teams make decisions together. Leadership, in other words, does not necessarily entail making every decision as the leader of a team. But it certainly does not require kicking every decision "upstairs."[29]

"We are striving to eliminate the conventional separation between strategic and execution roles that too often separate the thinkers from the doers," Hassan explains. "We also are seeking to eliminate as many layers as possible by fusing together ownership of the strategy with accountability for execution. We don't want clumsy or arbitrary decision-making. Each step is critical."

The new strategies at Schering-Plough produced results, beginning with compliance with the FDA consent decree. It involved thousands of individuals actions by hundreds of employees. "This new way of working is important because, as we've seen many times, how we work is what will drive long-term performance," Hassan said at a town hall meeting. "We have growing proof that this new way of working is delivering performance." Hassan pointed to the fact that the company had not had to make a single payment to the FDA for any missed deadlines, thanks to the actions of thousands of employees, as "evidence that the company has made strong progress on building quality compliance and business integrity into the DNA of the new Schering-Plough."[30] Hassan's new way of working included an active program of in-person meetings within various layers of the organization to encourage people to give him their frank and honest thoughts about what was working and what was not.

"Too often corporate philosophy is to deliver the numbers that will allow the company to be profitable," says Hassan. "Of course there are monetary rewards for quantitative results, but you have to look at the bigger picture. This includes compliance, ethics, and the long-term aspects of what you're doing. You have to be aware of the effect of what you do on other people. Your ability to contribute to organizational behavior is extremely important. It is also important to realize that even when you have made progress, there is always a lot of work ahead. You need to have a sense of humility, as well as passion, courage, and tenacity."[31]

Not As Easy As It Looks

Wishful thinking may be a seriously mistaken approach to business, but it's one that routinely captures CEOs who fall into the trap of maximizing short-term opportunities to profile their leadership in a positive light. These temptations only intensify when performance begins to falter. It takes courage to present the unvarnished truth when things aren't going well, particularly to a financial community that rewards CEOs for thinking only in the short-term and making their quarterly targets. It can be difficult to convince stakeholders of the value of taking a few hits today in the service of long-term success.

Some executives *never* admit the truth to themselves, taking their self-denials all the way to the courthouse, or even jail. Right up until his 2006 conviction on a number of charges, five years after Enron collapsed in a flurry of publicity about management misdeeds, former Enron chairman Kenneth Lay was still denying any wrongdoing, arguing that Enron had continued to deliver strong performance, being both profitable and achieving admirable growth, throughout its last days in 2001. According to Lay, "The Enron Task Force investigation is largely a case about normal business activities typically engaged in on a daily basis by corporate officers of publicly held companies throughout the country." He held on to the idea that Enron was "a real company, a substantial company that had a vision and values, a company that changed industries and markets for the better, a company that we were all proud to work for."[32] The rest of us, of course, now know better than that. Lay and former Enron CEO Jeff Skilling based their criminal trial defenses on these notions, and they lost. As Ann Tenbrunsel of the Institute for Ethical Business Worldwide puts it, "Self-deception causes the moral implications of a decision to fade, allowing individuals to behave incomprehensibly and, at the same time, not realize that they are doing so."

CEOs who create lasting success and strive to build trust can't afford to delude themselves into continuing to believe (and promote) a collective narrative that ignores the facts. Management must avoid wishful thinking at every juncture, drawing on the leadership qualities and infrastructure that make hard-nosed realism both possible and profitable.

CHECKLIST FOR AVOIDING WISHFUL THINKING

1. **Recognize that wishful thinking is a part of human nature.** It is a natural human tendency when confronted with information that contradicts your internal company story. Keep asking for the real story, even as you are assured you are receiving it. Monitor yourself for signs that you are not being as forthcoming as you should be. It takes courage to bring up vulnerabilities that are not yet apparent to anyone except you—but that are certain to become common knowledge eventually. Force yourself to confront reality.

2. **Use yourself as your own mirror, not the demands of others.** Realize that some stakeholders clamor for short-term positive news, which encourages wishful thinking right up until the minute it is proven wrong. Set realistic expectations. If stakeholders, including your board of directors, know what's coming, it will cushion the impact of bad news. If you are forthright, you can get people on your side.

3. **Invite honest criticism.** Set up systems that will ensure that bad news is brought to your attention. "Many leaders make it clear that they only want to hear the positives," says John Knapp, president of the Southern Institute of Business and Professional Ethics in Atlanta. "A brilliant approach is to assign a devil's advocate to bring this message to the CEO."[33] It should be the job of this executive-level employee to point out the weaknesses of internal plans and take the point of view of competitors.

4. **Build internal confidence.** People who feel confident can more easily reach out, work across functions, communicate honestly,

and not fear to disagree with management. Strong leaders, rather than creating fear of failure, are those who create the trust that honest communications is the value most prized in the organization. Of course, that requires ensuring that no one is punished, at any level, for sharing the truth as they see it.

5. **Reward transparency.** Establish new performance expectations and new metrics for measuring employee performance that reward transparency and openness. Bonuses, raises, or promotions, for example, can be tied to an employee's ability to make innovative suggestions and to work with other employees, particularly in different areas of the company, in order to create teamwork approaches to creating specific solutions.

6. **Share accountability and problem solving.** Instill a culture that recognizes shared accountability for solving problems. As Fred Hassan explains, "It's easy to point fingers and say it's somebody else's problem. In the end, the company suffers. Let's all own it if there is a problem."

7. **Listen and learn.** If you have an attitude of knowing all the answers, that you have "been there, done that," you've already begun to lose because nobody is going to help you. The most successful people are those who listen and learn, and therefore grow.

7

Riding the Technology Wave

All is flux; nothing stays still.

Heraclitus,
sixth-century B.C. Greek philosopher in *Diogenes Laertius,*
Lives of Eminent Philosophers

*Companies and countries who will thrive in the
Internet economy are those who change before the
rest of the world realizes that they have to change.*

John Chambers,
Chairman and CEO, Cisco Systems[1]

THE SUCCESS OF any business is linked to its ability to anticipate
and adapt to changing business conditions. For many companies,
the pace of technological change is the most important factor influ-
encing whether they can stay on top of intensifying competition and
new customer demands. According to a Gallup International survey
of 50,000 people in sixty-eight countries, 40 percent of respondents
rated "advances in technology" as the most important global challenge to which the business environment must adapt.[2]

Indeed, frequent seismic shifts in customer demand, combined
with radical technological change, have created a discontinuous pattern that is upsetting to many companies. As Lawrence H. Summers,

former president of Harvard University, commented at the 2006 World Economic Forum (WEF) in Davos, Switzerland, "disruptive new technologies are revolutionizing the global economy."[3] That's because in these times of rapid change, when companies need to respond quickly to unanticipated events, the past is no longer a very good predictor of future success. The numbers from previous quarters are no longer as valuable as they were in times of stability for controlling how companies behave. As Martin Sorell, CEO of the communications group WPP, commented at the same WEF brainstorming session in Davos, "It is almost impossible for traditional companies with traditional structures to adapt quickly enough."[4]

According to Bill Huyett and S. Patrick Viguerie of the consulting firm McKinsey & Company, the "topple rate" at which companies lose their leadership position doubled in the twenty years prior to the mid-1990s as new technologies knocked off the dominant industry players.[5] Huyett and Viguerie call the current environment an era of "extreme competition," and they note that companies with seemingly dominant positions are particularly vulnerable. Just consider Apple, which almost collapsed as personal computing turned to the Windows-Intel platform; Hewlett-Packard, which swallowed Compaq; and IBM, which abandoned the personal computer, a revolution they had pioneered. It is not only technology companies that are facing this challenge. The newspaper industry is struggling to reinvent itself as the Web competes for classified advertising dollars and threatens their ability to deliver news in a timely manner.

Jonathan Schwartz, CEO of Sun Microsystems, is determined that this will not happen at his company. "Over my lifetime, I will consume roughly three times the power my parents consumed—," Schwartz says, "and they, roughly three times their parents. As that trend continues, energy efficiency will become a competitive advantage for Sun (alongside Toyota, Boeing, BP, and GE)—and an environmental imperative for governments and voters. You may not care about it in your den, but multiply your den by three million, and I guarantee you, there's a lot to care about. Whether you're in rural Minnesota or rural India."[6]

An Era of Discontinuity

Discontinuity is the price we pay for the accelerating pace of change in our hypercompetitive global marketplace. While intensifying competition creates an assortment of problems, it also creates opportunities. For those flexible enough to respond, these discontinuities offer the chance for increased profit and growth, but only after a new paradigm has been created. Instead of relying on the past, companies will have to rebuild from the customer outward. "What will better serve their needs? What will they want in the future that they are not yet aware of and which we can only dimly predict?" Such questions play havoc with command and control. In fact, they tend to make that traditional way of leading untenable.

Even in this new, more unsettled environment, leaders can use their current financial and asset position to predict where new areas of strength may lie. That's where they need to invest heavily, both financially and emotionally. As technology devastates markets and creates new opportunities, flexible companies move with the technology, or die from their inability to do so. Optimizing opportunities may require a company to move away from a core business closely identified with it. Apple Computer moved to iPods and soared, demonstrating new strengths and a renewed leadership position through its ability to reinvent itself with a single new product, generated from the single idea that there was a better way for consumers to take their music with them wherever they go. At the end of 2005, the iPod family of products accounted for more than 40 percent of Apple's revenues, outpacing computer sales, that until very recently had been the core of the company.[7] Apple is of course by no means the only well-known company whose business no longer corresponds to the products to which their name is linked. Corning moved from glass to plastics; Volvo from cars to trucks; IBM from hardware to "headware"; Xerox from copiers to consulting; Kodak from film to digital.

Staying Ahead of the Technology Curve

Riding the technological wave requires the trust of every stake-holder group, including:

1. Customers, who will buy into the solutions you are offering them only if they trust that your response will meet new needs that they themselves are only beginning to understand.
2. Employees, who need to remain motivated and who have an even higher need than customers do to trust you—but a lower motivation.
3. Banks and bondholders, who must have confidence that the company will remain financially viable.
4. Shareholders and the board of directors, who need to provide the flexibility and patience to readjust to a new reality.
5. Even competitors, especially small entrepreneurial start-ups from which much of innovation streams.

Trust is at the core of every successful response to discontinuity. Noted Harvard professor of management Clay Christensen has discovered though his research that even perfectly reasonable but disruptive innovations are likely to be distrusted. "Within the successful parent company, mocking is the rational response to ideas that challenge the way it does business," he observes. Christensen suggests that the capital markets are likely to respond the same way, and that the solution for companies with promising new ideas is to separate them from their day-to-day business and allow them to grow without a lot of corporate oversight and control. "Once outside, away from the skeptical culture of the established business, the opportunity becomes very clear," he says.[8] Trust your people, in other words, to be able to capitalize on the strength of a new idea and to thereby enable themselves to get ahead of the game and ride the technological wave.

Objectively, making the decision to move on to promising new areas of strength should not be that difficult. Capitalism, after all, is supposed to reward the bold, innovative company that anticipates and responds to its customers' changing needs. The reality is usually more difficult. Hanging on to lines of business, real estate, and especially people may be counterproductive, but getting rid of them may prove even more traumatic. A leader can easily fall into the trap of throwing money at problem areas when investing in strengths alone can mean a rather sharp break from the past. Investing in strengths requires the power to manage your instincts and your stakeholders' emotions.

To successfully manage breaks with the past, every stakeholder has to be willing to overlook the fond memories of previous successes. But according to Christensen, the more fundamental difficulty in moving smoothly from opportunity to opportunity as they arise is that companies that do try to incorporate significant discontinuous innovations into their product mix often suffer equally significant financial setbacks, at least in the short term. The most significant challenge is that there is really no way to predict the outcome. As Christensen points out, "Markets that do not exist cannot be analyzed: suppliers and customers must discover them together. Not only are the market applications for new technologies *unknown* at the time of their development, they are *unknowable*."[9]

"The evidence is quite overwhelming," Christensen maintains, "that even today's most successful companies had *no idea* what they were doing at first—they just had enough money left over after they got it wrong to make it right." He suggests that companies must start with "plans of learning and discovery" rather than "plans of execution" if they want to be successful in a new business or market. That is, start with a projection of where you want to be, make the assumptions needed to get there, and then design a plan to test whether those assumptions are valid. Only then will you be able to decide whether or not to invest in the new idea.[10]

"Plans of learning and discovery," of course, are not how most companies do business on a daily basis. Small, incremental changes are what give stakeholders a feeling of trust. Unless leaders carefully prepare stakeholders for the inevitable downturns as the company moves to a new way of doing business, a lessening of essential trust is difficult to avoid, but not impossible. Certain companies have managed disruption well, and others are likely to succeed at it, because they have capitalized on a variety of inner strengths. Others have failed because they are unable to figure out an appropriate strength to support the necessary innovation.

At the 2006 World Economic Forum, I participated in a workshop on open innovation along with Richard Levine, president of Yale University; Henning Kantermann, CEO of SAP; John Swainson, CEO and chairman of CA; and a number of other CEOs of smaller technology companies. In summarizing the group's discussions, Levine noted that there are three imperatives to managing innovation successfully. First, there must be a commitment to openness. Second, you have to have a clear understanding of your own business and competitive advantages—what you can and cannot share. And third, there must be recognition that the interface between innovators requires trust. That trust is built on a mutual understanding of the business model and face-to-face interactions.[11]

Changing the Business Model: Gaining Flexibility Through Candor

When Anne Mulcahy became president of Xerox in 2000, the company was synonymous with the copy machine that was a fundamental part of the life of every businessperson. At the same time, the company was facing a looming liquidity crisis ($148 billion in debt). Mulcahy knew she'd have to change the way Xerox did business. Despite its high visibility in the hardware copier segment, Xerox was going to change its product focus to create a greater presence in high-end printers and multifunction networked systems that print, copy, fax, and scan. Mulcahy would have to resize the company, slash costs, and embark on an aggressive asset disposition schedule that would greatly improve cash flow and the balance sheet. In addition, she would have to deal with an accounting scandal that resulted in one of the largest fines paid to the SEC up to that time.

In other words, Xerox, a household name, would have to tighten up its operations. In the fall of 2000 Mulcahy announced to the Street that she would even have to consider cutting the stock dividend. She boldly announced that Xerox would focus its growth strategy on new products and documents management services.[12]

But Mulcahy's predecessor had not prepared the market for such a transformational shift. The headlines the next day focused not on Mulcahy's aggressive plan to remake Xerox, but instead on her declaration, early in her remarks, that Xerox had "an unsustainable business model."[13] Xerox's stock price immediately plunged 26 percent as rumors began circulating about a bankruptcy filing.[14]

No one outside Xerox seemed to have listened to the end of Mulcahy's speech, when she declared, "We are not focused on restoring the Xerox of the past, but we are re-orienting our business model to win in the context of the realities we face in today's increasingly competitive marketplace. I would also like to underscore that we are acting with a sense of urgency."

Perhaps Mulcahy overestimated analysts' tolerance for bluntness. She did, however, immediately understand the urgency of doing everything in her power to make certain company insiders did not miss the thrust of her message. During the next twelve months she traveled more than 100,000 miles visiting Xerox employees, talking to them directly about the new direction she wanted to take the company.[15] "Visiting with Xerox people gives me the motivation to keep going," she said at the time. "They tell you these incredible stories."[16]

Mulcahy realized that as the top executive during a sharp turn her most critical task was to be as honest as needed about Xerox's corporate prospects, but at the same time reassuring, by disclosing the plan that was in place to turn things around. During these critical times, strong leaders need to prepare their employees and other stakeholders, including directors, to endure both volatility and disbelief until the sharp turn in the direction of the business takes hold. Mulcahy did that.

By the third quarter of 2004, two-thirds of Xerox's revenue came from products introduced over the previous twenty-four months. Tight cost controls had a positive impact on profitability. Under treasurer Rhonda Seegal the capital structure of the corporation was revamped, and contacts with credit agencies strengthened, for an eventual improvement in the company's ratings. The strategy is being vindicated by the Street, the stock price having tripled between December 2000 and February 2006.[17]

Patricia Riley, director of the Annenberg Research Network on Globalization and Communication at the University of Southern California, notes that executives like Mulcahy tend to get better results when times are tough than those with less collaborative communication styles. Engaging stakeholders at every level is critical when fundamental changes are being driven through the organization. "At the top level, people are talking with language that is very action-oriented, things like, 'We are trying to inject speed,' or 'We are engineering our success,'" says Riley. "A boss needs to be able to shift from using the language of speed and urgency to the language of inclusiveness: 'Here is what we are doing, and here's what we need you to do.'"[18]

"The key to successful communication," Riley explains, "is trying to understand what people need to hear and how they need to hear it, rather than what executives want to say. It shouldn't be hard to get feedback on what your employees understand. But while organizations are good at sending out their message, they're not usually that good at getting feedback—and listening to it."[19]

Is Extreme Competition Compatible with Sharing?

Scott McNealy of Sun Microsystems argues that in today's participation age, building communities and sharing intellectual resources are imperative steps toward creating new markets and new economic opportunities. McNealy underlines that sharing and authenticity are fundamental to building trust. In today's technology environment in which "far-flung marketplaces will be compressed into a single, seamless body, where the network will stitch everything and everyone together," "going it alone" will increasingly be impossible.[20]

Sun has adjusted its business model to optimize advantages from this new reality by moving to open sourcing for their products. Sun is giving away Solaris, Sun's operating system, and its source code for free to the world. CEO Jonathan Schwartz states, "The open source model creates the most attractive long-term business model for us. We place an ever-heightening focus on our dialogue with the community." For Sun, this goes beyond maintaining the existing dialogue to finding new constituencies. "Developers don't buy things, they join things," Schwartz comments. "Sun is focused on growing new customers and all such opportunities start at some point through a conversation. There's a dialogue starting every minute of every day. It's just a matter of joining in."

In one twelve-month period, Solaris had 4.2 million downloads. Sun's strategy begins by blending internal assets with external audiences, including intellectual property and best practices. By building trust, the company strives to build a community, one that will grow around Sun. The philosophy is that the company can close the gap with critical audiences by engaging and collaborating with thought leaders and decision makers both within and external to the organization.[21] Sun aims to grow and strengthen its leadership by powering the next era, the Participation Age, in which an open and competitive network expands opportunities for everyone and, in turn, drives increased demand and business opportunity for Sun.

Cisco—Capturing Innovation Through Seamless Interface of Acquisitions

Probably the best example of a company that has developed both an internal and external strategy for staying ahead of the constant waves of technological transformation is Cisco Systems. This company profoundly understands that creative entrepreneurs are often the source of new technological innovation, so it both partners with its competitors and maintains an aggressive acquisition strategy. "The threats to big companies come from disruptive new technologies and start-up firms," says Intel chairman Craig Barrett. "If you look at the challenges to established companies, they do not usually come from other established companies, but from start-ups."[22]

John Chambers, CEO and chairman of Cisco since January 1995, had worked at both IBM and Wang, so he knew what it meant to suffer a painful decline by not adapting to fast-paced technological change. At Cisco, Chambers was determined that the product line would be broad, and that he would pick the right strategic partners.

"Very few people in this industry partner well," says Dan Scheinman, Cisco's senior vice president for corporate development. "It's become a huge competitive advantage for us. It is better to partner than to compete. It allows time to market advantages."[23]

Cisco perfected a strategy of identifying start-up technologies, acquiring a leader in the field, and integrating that company into its business model. This turned into a constant search for the next wave of disruptive technology and the companies or talents that were active and in the lead. Chambers set aside insular thinking and put acquisitions and partnerships front and center of the company's approach to growth. This became the core of Cisco's competitive advantage, as acquisitions became a key tool for bringing in new skills and new technologies and for managing the ecosystem in which Cisco operated. "Acquisitions are our core advantage," says Scheinman. "It has been one of the things that allows us to differentiate, and to accelerate, particularly in markets in transition."

Chambers expected that some forays into new technologies would fail, but he was committed to experimentation with new technologies as the key driver of Cisco's ability to generate strong growth. He recognized that if he wanted to sustain double-digit growth and continue to build Cisco's leadership position, he would have to take risks. "I learned that if you do not stay ahead of trends, they will destroy you," and that "there might be people smarter than you, but if you combine skills and strategy, you can beat them."

Scheinman agrees. "You must take risks to succeed," he says. "If you do the same thing that everyone else does, you will get the same result." Scheinman points out that the successful deals more than compensate for the ones that don't work out so well. "But the greatest risk is the deal that we do not do," he says. "In order to move quickly and successfully, we have to be constantly listening to customers to anticipate where the next disruptive market opportunity will be, be networked with the venture capitalists and bankers, and be trusted by the start-ups and entrepreneurs. Success in a changing and fast-paced environment is all about understanding and trust."[24]

Cisco investigates markets in transition, then looks everywhere for a company intimately involved in that business. Often Cisco's own customers drive the exploration. "Sometimes, " says Schein-man, "a remark from a customer will circle in my head for days and provide the direction for new areas we can explore. Our goal is to open new markets for ourselves, and at the same time increase our customer satisfaction by enabling them to do new things."

Acquisition, Then Integration

Chambers, Scheinman, and the rest of the team at Cisco under-stand that acquiring the right company, one which will help it enter and possibly dominate an emerging market, is only the first step to-ward its successful integration. The next, equally important strategy is to gain the trust of the new company so that the acquisition's most important talent remains. After all, it was their expertise that at-tracted Cisco to the company in the first place.

The search for acquisitions puts a high value on personal chem-istry and a common vision. "Acquisitions are smoother if people like each other," says Scheinman. "If we are attacking a huge market, it helps if we can immediately work seamlessly as part of one team."

The crucial part of Cisco's integration strategy is making em-ployees of the new company immediately feel part of Cisco. Employ-ees in both companies are made to understand and see rapidly the benefits of the combination. Logos and business cards are changed almost before the ink is dry on the contract, and a senior manager from the acquired company is appointed as the integration team leader. Managers of acquired companies are not considered rivals, but contributors who can help build what is now one company. The process of integration is both social and organizational, which is why Cisco has been able to overcome the tendency of global companies to fall into a "not invented here mentality" when faced with collaborations outside their group.

"We aim to create a platform where people are happy to be with us," says Scheinman. "If we consider all of our acquisitions, about 50 percent of employees have stayed with us. We're viewed as an open place to work. People see that many of our top executives have come through an acquisition. They feel like they can make a difference at Cisco."[25]

Cisco made its first important acquisition in 1993 when it bought the LAN switching company Crescendo Communications for $97 million. During the next dozen years Cisco's revenues grew from $28 million to $25 billion, and in financial year 2005 Cisco hired an average of more than a thousand new employees every three months.

Cisco's integration prowess will be put to the test with its most recent acquisition, Scientific Atlanta, the world's second largest maker of set-top cable-television boxes. At $7 billion, the acquisition is by far Cisco's largest ever. The move is aimed at thrusting Cisco into the consumer market by giving it a powerful foothold in the integration of video, telephone, and data across a single home network. Cisco intends to blend earlier acquisitions, like Linksys and the Danish company KISS Technology, with Scientific Atlanta in order to compete with the likes of Microsoft, Motorola, and a range of other companies that are trying to have their say as consumers define how they want to access, store, and manage digital media. Linksys has a $1 billion business in home-based wireless routers that can turn phones into Internet-friendly tools, and KISS sells DVD recorders that can be connected to the Internet.

Chambers is nothing if not confident of Cisco's ability to successfully absorb Scientific Atlanta, despite the fact that the acquisition strays from its historic model of buying tiny start-ups located close to its San Jose, California, headquarters. Chambers, while acknowledging that it may take up to two years to completely integrate

Scientific Atlanta into Cisco, insists that "it is not a gamble at all. It's one of the safer moves we've made."[26]

Finding a Balance

Cisco's experiences notwithstanding, most companies have difficulty finding a balance in the technology sector between working with competitors and drawing boundaries around aspects of their own innovation which they believe they cannot share. The reactions to the lines drawn are often colored by relationships, image, and elements of trust, as both established companies and start-ups battle to gain ground on constantly shifting terrain.

Microsoft is an example of a company with a long history of insular behavior. For years it has struggled with antitrust suits in the United States and Europe, as critics argued that it used unfair practices to maintain its dominant position in computer software. The company's almost constant visibility reinforced its reputation as fierce and arrogant with competitors, as headlines across the globe so gleefully pointed out. In the United States, the case against Microsoft was finally settled, but European Union regulators continue to try to force Microsoft to open up its software to facilitate competition and innovation from open-source developers. Finally, after decades of resistance, Microsoft is taking steps to provide third-party access to its source code, although that hasn't quieted most of its European critics.

The Internal Logic of New Investments: Lessons from IBM

Sometimes even when you are doing well, you know you should make radical transitions because of the discontinuity you see on the horizon. Stellar leaders capitalize on strengths and values to ensure that changes are successful in the long run, recognizing that they are almost certain to cause short-term (or even medium-term) disruptions.

Coping with such an environment can be "an Alice-in-Wonderland-like nightmare," according to Richard Foster, former principal at McKinsey & Company. He points out that people you know suddenly appear completely different as "the weak become strong and the strong become weak." These upheavals present management with an "almost hallucinogenic trip through territory they think they know but are suddenly incapable of navigating."[27]

In the 1980s IBM management almost bankrupted the company trying to respond to the discontinuity caused by the personal computer revolution, which seemed to occur overnight. It would take an entirely new management team, under the leadership of Louis Gerstner Jr., to make IBM a player again by emphasizing engineering as the way to provide solutions. More recently, under the leadership of Sam Palmisano, IBM reinvented itself once again as it moved away from the PC business altogether to focus almost exclusively on customer-focused, total corporate solutions. Palmisano was determined to capitalize on the research and consulting capabilities IBM had developed over decades of selling both hardware and software. With a focus on advice giving and problem solving, IBM manipulated the discontinuity of a hardware-sales-based business into relying on its expertise in information technology for much of its revenue. IBM is betting its future that businesses will want to outsource their backroom operations to a company that has long been in the business of easing customers' computing problems. This will, according to Palmisano, free customers to concentrate on their own core businesses while allowing IBM employees to apply their specialized skills to the problem of effectively managing vast amounts of data. In what some observers have called "raising the IQ" of its services, IBM has expanded its outsourcing by acquiring a number of client services firms during the past few years, most notably Price Waterhouse Consulting with its 30,000 experts.[28]

IBM expects its biggest profits to come from what it calls "business performance transformation" and "business process outsourcing." These are the primary offerings of the Global Services Division, headed by Ginni Rometty. "Business-performance-transformation services is a market we believe we're unlocking because of the skills and capabilities we've amassed to date," says Rometty. "[This market] is not available to traditional IT competitors because of what's required to participate."[29]

IBM had been in this space for decades, and it set out to sell large clients on services it was uniquely qualified to deliver. Solutions are intended to be flexible enough to provide everything the customer needs and nothing they don't, from leasing computing space to solving major glitches in their operating methods to outsourcing entire departments of data-intensive functions. Rometty expects companies and their consultants to use IBM methods and resources to "reengineer and streamline" any part of the selling and general and administrative process.[30] Because of its unique global expertise, IBM has been able to blur the line between providing information technology services and strategic consulting, always with an emphasis on practical solutions.

IBM's break with the past is still, in the opinion of many observers, a huge gamble. As may be expected when a company is responding to discontinuity, the transition hasn't always gone smoothly. Not all customers have been particularly happy turning over their backroom operations to a third party, and many IT departments are fighting their leaders' decisions to do so. IBM will likely face ups and downs until customers catch up with its vision of the future. Indeed, in 2005 several large IBM customers, including JP Morgan Chase, Cable & Wireless, and Invensys, canceled outsourcing contracts worth billions to IBM. Some of those defections were no doubt also due to intensified competition from the likes of EDS, Computer Sciences Corporation, and Accenture.[31]

But IBM is doing a good job in convincing its stakeholders to go along for the ride. Net earnings have returned to pretransition levels, and the stock has rebounded, although it has struggled to return to its 2002 levels. Most important, employees are being engaged by top management in an effort to get them personally enthused about a reinterpretation of IBM's 1950s-era "Basic Beliefs" for a new century. CEO Sam Palmisano recognizes that it will take time to change minds—both inside and outside the company. He has spent the past several years transforming the way the company thinks and communicating those changes to employees. He has also made certain those communications run two ways; he instituted a values-based management system as the way to get employees and customers to respond quickly in a rapidly changing environment.

"You could employ all kinds of traditional top-down management processes, but they wouldn't work at IBM, or, I would argue, at an increasing number of twenty-first-century companies," Palmisano explains. "You just can't impose command-and-control mechanisms on a large, highly professional workforce. The CEO can't say to them, 'Get in line and follow me,' or 'I've decided what your values are.' They're too smart for that."[32]

Palmisano divides IBM's new agreed-upon values, which he anticipates every employee will be able to support, into three categories:

1. Dedication to each client's success
2. Innovation that matters—for IBM and the world
3. Trust and personal responsibility in all relationships

These values have helped IBM manage its transition in a number of tangible ways, not the least of which is a complete revamping of pricing. In light of the new "client-friendly, cross-IBM solutions," it made no sense to continue to allow each business unit to set its own prices using its own profit-and-loss analysis.

"This was nuts because it's our ability to offer everything—hardware, software, services and financing—that gives us our real advantage," says Palmisano.[33]

Palmisano wants to make certain that every client brings a profit to IBM, but he is dedicated to ensuring the client's success, too. He made sure his senior executives came up with a system that reallocated costs to profit centers while maintaining all three of the values he had established. "Now when we make a truly cross-IBM bid, we can optimize it for the client and for us," he says.

In a way, Palmisano is striving to refashion IBM into the Big Blue of old, when its consultants sold the answers to the mysteries of making data dance. But this time around, IBM isn't just selling hardware and software. Palmisano expects to capitalize on IBM's most respected strength: its talent for finding elegant solutions.

Converting Customers

One of the biggest roadblocks to responding effectively to discontinuity comes down to the old saw "Know your customer." But, ironically, sometimes the better you know your customers, the harder it is to respond to changes that threaten your company's core identity. The natural response to threats will be to focus even harder on your best customers, with the idea that maintaining the status quo is the surest way to maintaining profits. But what will help your current customers the most in the short term—a line extension, product improvement, or an acquisition of a complementary company, for example—will probably not change the dynamics of your business. But neither will those changes help you survive the discontinuities that every business will eventually face as customer tastes and needs change now, more rapidly than ever. Only rarely do companies plan ahead in ways that allow them to look for customers in places where they haven't been seen before. Yet that is where the answers to discontinuities are found.

A good example of a business responding well to discontinuities by finding previously unconsidered customers is the dental industry. As fluoride in water supplies virtually eliminated cavities in many communities, both dentists and toothpaste manufacturers looked to respond creatively. Dentists refilled the treatment chairs with people who had sound teeth but less than sparkling smiles. High-tech cleaning and teeth-whitening techniques became an important profit center at many dental offices. Dental product companies followed the trend by producing cheaper, over-the-counter whitening alternatives to fill a need that those customers had not even considered a few years earlier.

All companies, of course, want to create new products for new markets. Using your institutional orientation to enhance offerings to existing markets through segmentation and intensified customer focus is fine as long as the customer segments you treasure are growing or competition is not too intense. But many companies tend to get wrapped up in their own identities, as personified by their traditional customer base; they continue to pursue these identities even if it is no longer in their best interest to do so. We've all watched companies pursue shrinking customer bases, all the while wondering why they don't open their eyes to markets that could be profitably served if they were only noticed. The most forward-looking leaders will look for both new customers and new solutions for current customers in unexpected places. Often this will mean coming up with radically new ways to fulfill a newly defined customer need. Wouldn't it have been something if airlines in the United States had invested in teleconferencing capabilities, co-opting what has become a potent alternative for their most important customers? Focused as they were on moving bodies from place to place, rather than ideas, new solutions that changed the paradigm of their industry never even occurred to them.

At 7-Eleven, Interfacing with Vendors Without Boundaries

Rapid technological change touches virtually every business, not just those in the technology sector. One retailer, for example, that has done a good job in recent years of harnessing new technologies and adapting to lifestyle changes among its customers is the convenience-store chain 7-Eleven. Before that company's most recent transformation began, most customers in the United States were young blue-collar males in a hurry. Give them a six-pack, smokes, perhaps gas and a snack, and they were gone. To attract professional women and stay-at-home moms (frequent 7-Eleven shoppers in other parts of the world), then president and CEO Jim Keyes knew he had to change the image of his convenience stores by making them truly convenient for everyone, especially women. That meant stocking them with much more than milk, beer, and candy by adding other products, including fresh foods that female consumers would ordinarily purchase at a grocery store.[34]

Keyes invested considerable resources in technology to support a business transformation that he calls "centralized decentralization." He has largely succeeded in attracting several new classes of customers while at the same time better serving existing ones. Store managers are now given a great deal of leeway to decide for themselves which products will move best in their own stores. "We want to give mom-and-pop stores the freedom to sell Spam sandwiches in their area if they are popular—unlike McDonald's, where the products are so strictly controlled that you can't meet local needs," says Keyes.[35]

Corporate headquarters supports this independence by providing information systems and logistics to help stores make good decisions and to make sure their selections are delivered in an exceptionally timely manner. Getting fresh foods into more than 5,800 U.S. stores as often as twice a day is a much different proposition than stocking them with packaged goods, and was made possible only by a radical change in 7-Eleven's technology and logistics structure.[36]

The key to the company's entire response to the discontinuity of changing buying habits is based on creating new relationships. Keyes knows that providing for the needs of his new customer segments is only possible by creating trusting partnerships with key vendors. To show its good faith, 7-Eleven has been much more forthcoming than most companies in sharing real-time sales data and helping its suppliers to analyze it. Its proprietary data-sharing program, called "7-Exchange," helps key vendors understand which of their products sell well or poorly in which stores. It includes sophisticated tracking software that virtually eliminates stock outages and helps vendor partners successfully launch new products. While

keeping tight control over data that tracks customer store-to-store
behavior, 7-Eleven is generous with data that helps its vendors do a
better job of bringing sales into its stores. When Gatorade, for example, wanted to launch a line of new flavors called Gatorade X Factor,
7-Eleven helped it identify the 25 percent of its stores that sold the
most isotonic beverages. By telling Gatorade where the new product
was most likely to succeed, 7-Eleven made the new drink a winner
for both companies.[37]

Transparency and openness with vendors creates the kind of
give-and-take relationships that are vital to successfully transforming companies. Dealing with discontinuity is difficult enough without maintaining a hypercompetitive stance with everyone around
you. It may go against common sense and human nature to open a
company up to scrutiny at the very time it is feeling most vulnerable,
that is, when it is trying to respond to a perceived need to do business in a completely new way. But this is exactly the time when such
behavior is most vital.

In its efforts to save money and provide services in the most efficient manner possible, not only does 7-Eleven share information
with its vendors, it has also begun to outsource many of its operations. Keyes decided to act after observing how much his Japanese
stores were able to reduce costs by adapting the Japanese *keiretsu*
model of supply management. Using an "integrated web of suppliers," stores can generate substantial growth and profits simply by using resources more wisely. Keyes has subsequently put every
7-Eleven corporate activity on the table for possible outsourcing, retaining only those products and services which represent its "core"
and which the company does better or cheaper than any vendor
could. Its withdrawal from the distribution of fresh food, for example, has allowed it to reduce overhead and eliminate direct distribution costs while getting fresher foods into its store more frequently.[38]
By outsourcing other products, it has also become a "one-stop
source" for many nontraditional convenience store products, such
as check cashing.

"Any good business is always in the process of reinventing itself because customers are always changing," says Keyes. "Reinventing a business—changing its target markets—cannot be done with advertising, although some companies try. Instead, I'm a big believer in the appeal of the product. It's amazing how fast word travels when customer needs are anticipated.[39]

The Trust-Value Connection

Obviously, there is more than one way to respond to discontinuity and the pace of technological change. But regardless of which strategy you use, your response should be so apt, so in tune with the situation, that stakeholders respond with enthusiasm. You want them to give you enough breathing room and support so that you can go about the business of transforming your company or profit center without too much opposition. That means tapping into the trust-value connection. It means having the confidence to go beyond the denials that you will hear from entrenched interests, intuiting for yourself the subtle signs of change, and having the contextual intelligence to move before you are confronted with a major disruptive phenomenon. According to Rosabeth Moss Kanter, "the antidote" to this noise, which allows you to get a correct read from those around you, is "dialogue—the capacity to discuss the undiscussable."[40]

Gaining the trust of your stakeholders during times of change is an invaluable asset. Every communication about your transformation must convey your vision of how the transformed company will look, the progress it has made, and the support it is receiving from stakeholder groups. Stories such as these, told repeatedly, take on the ring of truth even before they are fully grasped. As long as you are making progress, and your strategy appears to have logical underpinnings, you can receive at least grudging support for your efforts, support that is likely to develop into trust as your ideas start bearing fruit.

CHECKLIST FOR MANEUVERING THROUGH DISCONTINUITY

1. **Disruption as an Opportunity.** Lead the organization to view discontinuous patterns in technological change not as a frightening disruption, but as an opportunity.

2. **Sustain the trust of your key stakeholders.** Recognize that to drive change within your organization, you will need employee trust to sustain motivation. Support from shareholders and the board will also be essential to provide time to readjust to a new reality. And solidify relationships with competitors, especially small entrepreneurial start-ups, from which so much of the innovation comes.

3. **Invest in strengths, not weaknesses.** Too many companies spend too much money trying to fix problems. A more productive approach is to concentrate fully on your company's strengths. This is not "core competencies" that you do well, but what you can do better than anyone else. Cut problem areas loose sooner rather than later.

4. **Listen, but be one step ahead.** Listen to what your employees are saying about the company's strengths, weaknesses, and values. But here's a radical thought: Don't listen to your customers with a focus only on satisfying their current needs. Look for emerging concerns and solutions they may not yet be aware of.

5. **Look for growing customer segments in unexpected places.** Do a little "opposites attract" thinking. Who is the very opposite of your current customer? Where is there a promising, dynamic market that you have not tapped? In the case of 7-Eleven, it was the busy soccer mom, the antithesis of the young, single beer drinker. What could you offer that opposite customer? You may have to do it one day to survive, but even if you never go down this road in reality, the exercise will get you thinking the right way to manage discontinuity successfully.

8

Engage in the Public Policy Game

For, in the final analysis, our most basic common link is that we all inhabit this small planet. We all breathe the same air. We all cherish our children's future.

John F. Kennedy[1]

What "vegetable" do American infants and toddlers eat most? Weep, for it's the french fry.

Nicholas D. Kristof,
The New York Times[2]

© Susan Andrews of Andrews & Braddy Studio, Inc.

WHEN WE HEAR the word "lobbying," what often comes to mind are corrupt attempts to influence government officials. That's because the news pages often profile lobbyists who have pleaded guilty to fraud or conspiracy to bribe public officials. This has tarred the reputation of lobbying, which is not necessarily the same as the corporation's valid task of engaging in the debate about social and political issues that affect their business.

Executives broadly agree that they *should* engage on the political front. A December 2005 survey by *The McKinsey Quarterly* of 4,238 executives in 116 countries clearly shows that executives around the world overwhelmingly embrace the idea that the role of corporations in society goes far beyond simply meeting obligations to shareholders and that the effective management of sociopolitical concerns is so important that it must start with the CEO.[3]

"More than four out of five respondents," the survey goes on to report, "agree that generating high returns for investors should be accompanied by broader contributions to the public good—and an equal commitment to minimizing negative effects of business. Only one in six agrees with the thesis, famously advanced by Nobel laureate Milton Friedman, that high returns should be a corporation's sole focus."

In the same study, almost no one—a minimal 3 percent—felt that even large companies did a good job of anticipating social pressure and criticism. According to Lenny Mendonca, a director at McKinsey & Company, companies often end up with "a reactive and tactical response, rather than a strategic one."[4] As a result, even those executives who try to respond to social concerns are frustrated that their companies may be taking the wrong approach. For example, almost half (48 percent) of those surveyed said that companies in their sector lobbied government and regulators, but only a quarter believed those efforts to be effective.

Of the more than 11,000 public companies in the United States, only about 1,000 make any effort at all to influence government policy. Most of those that do are the largest multinationals, many of whom employ small armies of lobbyists and a range of public relations tactics. But as the McKinsey survey illustrates, even these companies, with all their firepower, often struggle to effectively contribute to or anticipate shifts in public policy. One reason is that, at most compa-

The Role of Business in Society

% of respondents[1]

Which of the following statements best describes the role that large corporation (public and private) should play in society?

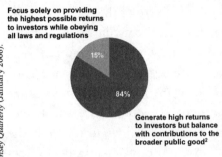

Focus solely on providing the highest possible returns to investors while obeying all laws and regulations

15%

84%

Generate high returns to investors but balance with contributions to the broader public good[2]

Which of the following statements best describes the overall contribution that large corporations (public and private) make to the public good?

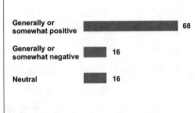

Generally or somewhat positive — 68

Generally or somewhat negative — 16

Neutral — 16

[1] All data weighted by GOP of constituent countries to adjust for differences in response rates from various regions.
[2] For example, by providing good jobs, making philanthropic donations, and going beyond legal requirements in minimizing pollution and other negative effects of business.

nies, making the case to governing bodies and critics is relegated to a department several layers down in the organization, without much personal involvement by top management. It often adds up to little more than "influence peddling," taking a short-term view that aims to protect a company's entrenched position rather than play a role in the political debate.

Why do tens of thousands of companies make no effort at all to engage in the public policy debate that affects their interests? It could be that most of them, particularly if they are small or medium-sized firms, feel they cannot influence outcomes or manage socio-political pressures. They are very much like citizens who never participate in the political process, even though political decisions can profoundly affect their lives. Political scientists call the actions of such consumers "rational ignorance," the notion that it is logical to ignore things that impact your life but cannot be changed by your actions.[5] But even Google, viewed as the protypical "outsider," recently hired a team of lobbyists. Caught in a wave of criticism about its policies in China and questions about the privacy of people's Internet searches, Google determined it needed to engage in the Washington debate about the open Internet platform.

When it comes to public corporations, however, not participating in the political process amounts to "irrational ignorance." It is irrational because oftentimes corporate executives have more influence than they think, regardless of the size of their company. As a leader, your options are severely limited if you allow rules or settlements to be imposed from the outside, whether by lawsuit, new laws, or changes in the regulations affecting your company. They are also limited if you have no voice in how government is responding to changing public sentiment. It's much more effective to anticipate the waves of change coming your way and try to be the first in your industry to head off in a more promising new direction.

Gerber Takes a Stand

One company that has taken the lead in the public policy debate affecting its business is the Gerber Products Company. Founded in Dorothy Gerber's kitchen in 1928, Gerber is now the world's most prominent name in baby foods. Back in 2002 there were recommendations from various expert groups, but no comprehensive set of dietary guidelines, that addressed the unique nutrition and feeding issues of children under two. But while no one had yet looked at the impact of very early childhood nutrition on the fitness of older children and adults, Frank Palantoni, Gerber CEO at the time, felt it was only a matter of time before sociopolitical pressures began to influence governments to start taking a closer look at the nutrition requirements for young children. In fact, because the long-term effects of children's poor eating habits incurred lifelong health-care costs, many governments had already begun an intensified effort to lay the blame for childhood obesity on both food companies and public policy. First Lady Laura Bush soon began calling for healthier foods in schools, numerous school boards began agitating for the removal of snack-vending machines, and governments around the world were considering legislation to restrict the marketing of certain food products to children.

It was a McDonald's advertisement depicting an infant with a french fry that galvanized Palantoni into action. He was outraged that marketing tactics were being used to encourage parents to feed their infants french fries. He was determined that Gerber would take a leadership role on the topic of childhood nutrition, influence the debate, and play a visible role in setting standards based on scientific study. Because of the company's large database on childhood eating patterns and its leading share of the infant nutrition market, Gerber was superbly positioned to step up and help shape the public policy debate about how to improve the dietary habits of babies and children. "We feel our role in American society, as it pertains to health, is that we have a responsibility to be a leader in infant nutrition," said Palantoni.[6]

"Gerber already had a stellar identity as a baby food company," agrees current president and CEO Kurt Schmidt. "We wanted to use that identity to get out front on a public policy debate so that the issue would help, not hurt the company."[7]

In spring 2002 Gerber sponsored the largest-ever dietary intake survey of infant and toddler nutrition, involving 3,000 babies between the ages of four months and two years. Gerber believed that this was the critical but often ignored period when a child's tastes and preferences are shaped. The purpose of this Feeding Infants and Toddlers Study (FITS) was to investigate infant and toddler food choices and nutrient intakes, and determine whether the Institute of Medicine's* standards for vitamins and minerals were being met. The results, released in October 2003 at an annual conference of the American Dietetic Association in San Antonio, Texas, were startling. It found that infants and toddlers as young as four to six months were consuming too many calories and eating inappropriate foods. Although these foods met their vitamin and mineral requirements,

---

*The Institute of Medicine was chartered in 1970 as a component of the National Academy of Sciences.

many babies showed signs of the unhealthy diet adopted by much of
the American adult population. For example, the study found that:

1. Soda was being served to infants as young as seven months.
2. On any given day, nearly 25 percent of 19–24-month-old
   babies did not eat a single fruit or vegetable.
3. By 19–24 months, many toddlers consumed sweets, desserts,
   or salty snacks at least once a day.
4. Among those 19–24 months, the french fry was the most
   commonly consumed vegetable.

FITS was the first comprehensive study to document that children were consuming empty calories in desserts, sweets, salty snacks,
french fries, and carbonated beverages at shockingly early ages. The
findings seemed to confirm that American children were in real danger of growing up to become a part of an obese generation. In a related study, sponsored by Gerber, seven out of ten parents in the
study had no idea how many fruits and vegetables to feed their children daily, and 43 percent reported that their child had eaten a
french fry by the age of one. A study that Gerber had sponsored earlier at the University of Tennessee confirmed the importance of early
food preferences in shaping lifelong eating habits.

Armed with these findings, Gerber launched Start Healthy, Stay
Healthy, a research, education, and media campaign, to promote
better eating choices for babies. It featured practical help to parents
about making healthy eating choices for their children. To launch
the campaign, Gerber placed a two-page advertisement in *Time* magazine of a blue-eyed baby boy holding a french fry. "Bad eating habits
are learned early," read the headline. "Sure, it's tempting to let your
baby eat convenient adult foods," the ad continued. "But now is your
best opportunity to teach good eating habits."

In the month after Gerber launched Start Healthy, Stay Healthy,
Gerber's 800 number for health-care professionals generated 11,000
requests for information, and the Gerber hotline experienced a fif-
teenfold increase in calls from physicians. On the product side, Ger-

ber launched a line of organic baby foods, freeze-dried 100 percent fruit snacks, "Mini fruits," and tot-sized microwavable healthy dinners. Called Lil Entrées, they resemble miniature TV dinners, and each provides a serving of vegetables.

Health care and the health of American children in particular remains high on the political agenda. Headlines pointing out that babies born in the United States are less likely to survive their first year than babies born in Slovenia[8] increasingly grab the attention of the public and elected officials. As part of an effort to improve childhood health, public pressures continue to mount to tax junk food and to ban sodas, potato chips, and other such snacks from schools.

Gerber was one of the first companies to act, and its executives took a tack that allowed them to engage in "constituency building," leveraging "beneficial linkages between political strategies and market-based strategies," says Wake Forest management professor Michael D. Lord. "This can help enhance the competitive advantages of both. Firms with quality products, satisfied employees, and happy and loyal customers can leverage these assets toward favorable public affairs and powerful political influence. In contrast, all the money, public relations, and lobbyists in the world may do little to help advance a firm's public policy interests if they have a poor corporate reputation, dissatisfied workers, and disgruntled customers."[9]

Companies like Gerber and Campbell Soup begin with the advantage of a positive perception in the minds of consumers. "We're fortunate that our main business has an inherent health orientation and perception," says M. Carl Johnson III, chief strategy officer and senior vice president at the Campbell Soup Company. "So we fortunately start with a much stronger position than some of our peer group." But Campbell has also made it a point to establish strong relationships with government bodies like the Food and Drug Administration and the U.S. Department of Agriculture, and with major health organizations like the American Heart Association, the American Dietetics Association, and the American Association of Pediatrics. "We help them understand the industry and what's scientifically possible and not possible," says Johnson, "and in some cases we actually partner with them. We'll also reach out to various interest groups, some of whom may not be historically friendly to the industry." Examples include cosponsorship, along with Nike, McNeill Labs, and the U.S. Surgeon General of an initiative called Shaping America's Youth, and the online Campbell Center for Wellness and Nutrition. To Johnson, public policy and corporate strategy are inseparably linked. "One of our guidelines is that we can't do a new product that doesn't have a stated nutrition strategy to it," he explains.[10]

In other words, doing the right thing can be wonderfully compatible with profitable marketing. Gerber, and the vast majority of companies of every size and in every industry worldwide, operate in a business environment in which they must endeavor to set the agenda—or be ready to comply with whatever constraints activist regulators increasingly impose on them. Indeed, a global effort to force food companies to help combat the obesity problem may be gaining traction. After a 2005 study showed startling growth in weight problems among European children, the European Commission threatened to legislate a ban on advertising junk food to children unless the food industry ended the practice voluntarily. The commission also began pressing for plain-language nutrition labels, and in Britain the government is considering requiring warning labels on products found to cause weight gain in children.[11]

An Agenda Founded on Engagement

Companies have always tried to influence public policy, of course, but in today's globalized environment the stakes of the game, as well as the game's complexity, have been raised. Even small companies today who do business around the world may be subject to new challenges and regulations in the countries in which they operate. When companies attempt to engage in actions designed to influence public policy (ranging from political contributions to actually shaping the agenda), it is not simply because they want to be lavished with special favors. Rather, it is an outgrowth of the hard realities of consumer activism and political pressures in a world with instant information flow. Criticism comes from multiple sources, often organized and linked with powerful networks. The impact on policy and politicians is profound. A poll of those attending the World Economic Forum in Davos, Switzerland, in early 2006 found that 63 percent of the CEOs surveyed believed that politicians were too sensitive to the pressures of public opinion.[12]

In the United States, the states themselves are assuming more responsibility for regulating corporations, particularly as the federal government under Republican leadership philosophically objects to most government regulation. In May 2005 Connecticut's General Assembly voted to remove sugary soft drinks and some junk foods from public schools, including lunchrooms and vending machines.[13] It would have been the strictest ban in the United States, but after an aggressive lobbying effort by the American Beverage Association, among others, Connecticut Governor M. Jodi Rell vetoed the measure, despite the fact that a statewide opinion poll conducted by the Connecticut Center for Research and Analysis found that 70 percent of people in Connecticut favored a school soda ban. Bowing to public sentiment, the ABA, backed by PepsiCo and Coca-Cola, introduced a voluntary ban on all drinks except water and 100 percent juice in elementary schools in the United States, and a ban on all full-calorie soft drinks in middle schools. More recently, advocacy groups have filed suit in Massachusetts against Viacom and Kellogg to stop them from marketing junk food to young children. They particularly object to Kellogg licensing its cartoon characters from the Viacom-owned kids cable channel, Nickelodeon, to create such products as SpongeBob SquarePants Wild Bubble Berry Pop-Tarts.

Meanwhile, in Washington at least one legislator is taking aim at the $10 billion that food companies spend annually marketing to children. Senator Tom Harkin of Iowa has announced that if the food industry is unwilling to meaningfully police this kind of advertising on its own, he would introduce legislation to impose federal regulation. "Parents' choices about their children's eating habits are undermined by junk food ads every day," says Harkin. "Although parents want their kids to eat healthy, they often lose out because . . . cartoon superheroes entice kids to eat fast food and sugary snacks. The childhood obesity epidemic is real and the time to act is now."[14]

The fact that Harkin is a Democrat in a Republican Congress may be reassuring to some food company executives. But his crusade should be seen for what it really is: a public policy wake-up call. Even legislation that goes nowhere is an indication of churning grassroots sentiments that may soon grow to haunt certain companies. Clearly, the issue calls for monitoring, engagement, and active dialogue. As activism increases, and in the context of our litigious society, companies are much more likely than ever to be sued over practices outsiders find questionable. These lawsuits can also become triggers for social or political action. McDonald's, for example, is facing a slew of lawsuits concerning the healthiness of its products, including one celebrated suit accusing it of misleading children about the healthiness of its food. *Pelman vs. McDonald* was filed on behalf of two teenagers alleging that McDonald's had deceived them by running advertisements claiming its products were nutritious and could easily be part of a healthy lifestyle. The teenagers also alleged that the company failed to make nutritional information available in all its restaurants. The case was originally thrown out by the lower courts, which ruled that the plaintiffs had failed to show that McDonald's products posed any danger that was "not within the common knowledge of consumers." But in 2005 a U.S. Appeals Court allowed the case to be reopened, which has led some observers to speculate about the possibility of huge tobacco-like lawsuits against food companies.

Other companies, too, now seem to be acknowledging the handwriting on the wall. Kraft, for example, has announced a ban on marketing to kids and in January 2005 launched a series of ads showing kids seriously discussing nutrition. Both these decisions, however, had the late-to-the-party feel that may not serve these companies well in the long run. Stakeholders tend to know the difference between reluctant acquiescence to threats and an enthusiastic, early embracing of an issue of concern to the public. Companies will gain more trust—and more political capital to use later—by engaging in social issues from the start and from the early adoption of obvious public policy trends. Indeed, studies have shown that companies can increase their chances of achieving credibility with their customers and getting what they want from the political process—and even from the courts—by making themselves stand out from their competitors with a clear voice.[15] The best way to do that is to embrace emerging opportunities, which in turn facilitates a more meaningful public debate. The rules have changed, and companies must get out in front if they want to help shape the dialogue. If the public, or any other key stakeholder for that matter, is suddenly concerned about the negative aspects of a company's business practice or product, that company would be wise to concern itself with it as well. Developing a strong public statement, or better yet a proactive initiative, to combat the underlying societal problem will go a long way toward establishing trust. And the more mold-breaking the solution, the more leeway a company will receive from those who have been convinced to try to legislate, regulate, or litigate away the latest crisis.

Anticipating, Taking Charge of Change

The tales of Coke and Pepsi in the obesity wars illustrate how timely action can either turn aside or accelerate government action. As local school boards and municipalities became concerned about the food and drinks it was offering to their children, Coke initially did not change its marketing in schools despite consumer agitation. Many schools across the country began to remove Coke products from their vending machines. PepsiCo reacted to the outcry over overweight children with an effort to engage in finding a solution. It reduced the portion sizes of its school vending-machine products to reduce calories by half, and restricted its advertising to children, agreeing not to promote many of its products, including certain snack foods, with kid-friendly advertising.[16]

CEO Steven Reinemund has also committed PepsiCo to a new line of foods called Smart Spot, with a proprietary labeling system developed by an independent advisory board of health experts intended to help consumers easily identify healthy food choices. The Smart Spot symbol can now be found on about one hundred PepsiCo products, including Tropicana juices, Gatorade, Baked Lays potato chips, Quaker Oatmeal, and Diet Pepsi. The Smart Spot criteria includes limits on the amount of saturated and trans fats, cholesterol, sodium, and added sugar. It also serves to identify products using reduced amounts of these ingredients, as well as those formulated to have specific health or wellness benefits.[17]

"We've committed to achieving more than half of our new product revenues from Smart Spot products in North America," says Reinemund. "We're also stepping up efforts in our new product pipeline to capture this opportunity in markets around the world."[18]

In another example of good citizenship intersecting with good business, sales of these healthier products are growing at more than twice the rate of those without the Smart Spot label, and are the fastest growing part of Pepsi's North American product portfolio. In early 2006 Reinemund announced that PepsiCo would dedicate half its annual snack food advertising budget to promoting healthier products, an increase of more than 50 percent.

With Smart Spot and its strategy of emphasizing products with less salt, sugar, and fat, Pepsi was responding to public and government sentiment. By moving fast, the company gained market share at the expense of its chief competitor, Coca-Cola. Between 1996 and 2004, PepsiCo was diversifying into healthy snacks, water, and juices. At that point Coke remained focused on carbonated brands. During this period, PepsiCo increased profits by more than 110 percent, while profits at Coca-Cola increased only 38 percent. In early 2006, Coca-Cola began taking full-page advertisements in national newspapers announcing in large letters, "Your needs have changed. Your tastes have changed. And the Coca-Cola Company is changing right along with you."[19] The ad went on to announce its commitment to "products that answer your needs," "supporting physical activity," "helping you make informed choices about nutrition," and "listening to your wishes in our advertising practices."

Reinemund directly attributes PepsiCo's recent financial performance to its embrace of health and wellness. "Politicians expect us to be on the defensive when we talk about health and wellness, but we're not," he said shortly after the introduction of Smart Spot. "It's a huge opportunity to build new brands and markets."[20]

It Doesn't Take a Genius

Virtually every company, in virtually every industry, would be best advised to keep a close watch on the public policy debate. Sooner or later, what's being talked about in city hall, in Congress, and at the watercooler is going to have a significant impact on your business.

For example, the latest hot button related to the latest energy crisis is not only concern about the price of a gallon of gasoline, but, more important, America's reliance on foreign oil. Yet there is only one automobile manufacturer that has taken advantage of this debate by, through its actions, being perceived as the leader in manufacturing environmentally responsible automobiles. Toyota has accomplished this by introducing an impressive line of fuel-efficient hybrid vehicles.[21]

It doesn't take a genius to understand that the price of gasoline is trending upward, and that western countries' reliance on foreign oil will be an important political issue for the foreseeable future. It does, however, take a special kind of company to move to change concretely its business in order to seize an opportunity. After selling about 250,000 hybrid vehicles globally last year, Toyota is targeting sales of 400,000 units in 2006, with the addition of versions of the Lexus LS and Toyota Camry hybrids to add to its popular Prius model.[22] According to R. L. Polk & Co., a Michigan firm that collects and interprets automotive data, hybrids could make up to 35 percent of the U.S. market by 2015.[23]

Toyota is, of course, not the only automobile company committed

to selling hybrids. Honda, too, has entered the market in a significant way, manufacturing Civic, Accord, and Insight models that currently make up about 30 percent of the market share of hybrids.
Ford is also trying to be a player, having introduced the Ford Escape,
the first hybrid sports utility vehicle. It is also responsible for introducing the first hybrid made in the United States, bringing hybrid
technology to the American manufacturing process for the first time.
But for the most part, U.S. car companies are perceived as being late
to the market—followers, not leaders. Consumers, politicians, and
the media all flock to a winner. Of the early adopters of hybrid technology, Toyota has clearly given itself a big head start, earning a
"halo . . . as a leading green manufacturer," according to journalist
John Griffiths of *The Financial Times*.[24]

Years before the first Prius entered the showroom, Toyota anticipated that as world oil supplies were threatened and as the geopo-
litical environment intensified, gas prices would continue to rise,
placing pressure on both consumers and governments to conserve
energy. The leadership at Toyota envisioned that a certain kind of
consumer—socially conscious—would be a natural market for the
Prius. But they knew, based on their experience in high-priced gasoline markets in Japan and elsewhere, that many customers who
weren't even necessarily environmentally conscious would be willing
to consider the hybrid solution. So Toyota bet big on the Prius, putting marketing muscle behind it and hustling hybrids into show-
rooms.

In the process of using hybrids to solidify its position as the
most important automaker in the United States, Toyota is using its
influence to great advantage. While General Motors, long the main-
stay of Michigan's auto industry, closes plants and sends jobs out of
the country, Toyota is building two more American factories. That
is the kind of success that attracts the attention of even cash-
strapped state governments. No wonder Michigan Governor Jennifer Granholm didn't fear voter retribution when in the spring of
2005 the state gave Toyota $39 million in tax breaks to open a new
R&D center in Ann Arbor.[25]

Can Elephants Really Dance?

For decades it has been an article of faith among Republican leaders that less regulation is good, more regulation is bad. Just get government off their backs has been their political mantra, and American businesses will prosper. But corporate scandals have severely tested that philosophy, as new rules have had to be put in place to protect corporate shareholders from fraudulent financial reporting. Indeed, the United States is slowly entering an era when increased regulation is going to be more frequently imposed by politicians who want to be seen as acting decisively to clean up corporate excesses. Politicians at all levels—federal, state, and local—want to be seen as "doing something" about the bad apples whose profit-at-all-costs misadventures have made headlines.

Companies are recognizing that when they face new regulations, playing by rules that they've had a hand in formulating makes it easier to navigate the new path. While the McKinsey study found that business executives overwhelmingly believe that corporations should balance their obligation to shareholders with explicit contributions "to the broader public good," most executives view their engagement with the corporate social contract as a risk, not as an opportunity. They frankly admit that they are ineffective at managing wider social and political issues."[26]

Some companies, Gerber, Toyota, and BP among them, have thrived by taking a public, responsible stand on an important sociopolitical issue. These companies have proved that despite its reputation as a cost center with no tangible benefit in terms of income gained or losses averted, a forward-looking public policy strategy makes complete sense from the profit-and-loss perspective alone. There is financial benefit from engaging in public affairs correctly. So much the better when it can also enhance your reputation as a responsible corporate citizen.

Jeffrey Immelt readily admits that General Electric's Ecomagination pro-environment initiative is a pitch to customers, employees, and regulators. In a May 2005 speech at George Washington

University during which he launched Ecomagination, Immelt pledged to double GE's research on environmentally friendly technologies, such as wind power, hybrid locomotives, and water purification. He also promised to reduce GE's greenhouse gas emissions by one percent by 2012, a sharp reversal of the company's projections that they would jump 40 percent during that period if no improvements were made.[27]

For GE, it's also about making money from the environment, and Immelt makes no bones about that. That's what makes capitalism so effective. Innovations like solar power and alternative fuels will gain traction only when they are financially viable, not by government fiat or wishful thinking, but because customers want them.

"Ecomagination is a new concrete commitment by GE to develop and drive technologies of the future that will protect and clean our environment, innovate to promote energy efficiency, lower emissions, reduce our use of fossil fuels, and increase the supply of usable water," says Immelt. " We believe we can improve the environment and make money doing it. We see that green is green."[28]

Indeed, many of the products GE sells, such as coal gasification turbines, help customers, particularly utilities, reduce their CO_2 emissions. Immelt expects the turbine business to generate $1 billion in revenues for GE as government litigators like New York State attorney general Eliot Spitzer become more aggressive about combating pollution.

Immelt feels the same way about international regulations, welcoming them as good for business. He wants to increase the demand for GE's pollution-fighting products in other countries, particularly China and India, and he supports the Kyoto protocol because, as he put it after the Ecoimagination launch, "having global standards makes business easier."[29]

Maintaining a Trust-Building Public Affairs Operation

Companies like Gerber, BP, GE, and Toyota, which have been able to find financial profit in getting ahead of the public social policy discussions, also have the opportunity to engage in the debate. When BP executives talk about global warming, or Gerber talks about child nutrition, or when Cemex talks to the Mexican government about recyclable energy, people listen. Yet many new-generation corporate executives are reluctant to engage in a public policy debate on issues that affect their business, choosing instead to weigh in only when their business is threatened.

Doug Schuler, an expert on corporate political activity at the Jesse Jones Graduate School of Business at Rice University, maintains that public affairs efforts are not really high on the list of priorities at most companies "until an issue jumps up and bites them." "A midsize U.S. box company is probably not going to be interested in trade policy until Chinese boxes start coming in and competing," he explains. "Too many companies treat public policy as exogenous. To them, it's like the weather—they just react to it. But policy making is social construct with actors. Even small and medium companies can participate if they pick their issues wisely. They need to realize that they are one of those actors, and they can play the game."[30]

Starbucks chairman Howard Schultz learned this lesson during his first visit to Washington in 2004. Schultz considered Starbucks a different kind of company, more interested in treating its workers and suppliers with respect and brewing an exceptional cup of coffee than currying special favor with politicians. He felt much more comfortable talking about Starbucks' experience in providing health insurance for all its workers than about coffee tariffs or tax policy or anything else specifically skewed to Starbucks' business and profitability. Lawmakers were taken aback by the "soft sell," but Schultz soon got a lesson about the benefits of becoming directly engaged in public policy that will affect profitability.

As Congress was hammering out the voluminous 2004 tax bill, Starbucks was in danger of losing its ability to deduct a portion of the cost of roasting and packaging green coffee beans. That deduction was worth millions to the company. Starbucks had only recently established its own lobbying office in Washington, and the head of government affairs, Kris Engskov, made the case for retaining the status quo. Intense discussions—with a bit of arm-twisting—resulted in what would actually be called the "Starbucks exemption" being added to the bill before passage, and the company's deduction was preserved.[31] Starbucks now has little compunction about fighting for its own agenda, such as brand protection in China and lower tariffs overseas, as it continues on a parallel track to support the social policies it believes are valuable.

Turning Challenges into Opportunities

Corporations are operating in a world of reputational risk in which the trust of governments, and certainly the trust of the consumer, is central to the successful operation of virtually every business. Finding trust-enhancing ways to influence public policy cannot be simply ceded to internal public affairs or lobbyists alone. Leaders of any organization must take personal responsibility for making certain that trends in legislation, regulation, litigation, and public activism are spotted and acted upon.

The most obvious way to do just that is to monitor public policy and regulatory developments in every country, state, and locality in which you do business or might do business in the future. Many executives believe that the public affairs or lobbying function is only a cost center whose duties can be delegated to a trade association or lobbying firm. Not so. Engagement in public affairs should be approached as part of corporate strategy, with input from top management. Even divisions of midsize companies can benefit from assigning a person or two to the task of monitoring the public policy environment. When Starbucks' tax deduction was threatened by the initial draft of the 2004 tax bill, the first step toward getting it corrected was to simply understand that a change was being proposed. The next step was to enlist the help of senators from states where Starbucks had roasting plants. A few lines in a new public law can have a significant effect on a company's fortunes, and can be influenced by just one or two local politicians.

In recognition of the potential value or harm of government actions, the diversified international company Cargill has actually established a measurement system to track the tangible benefits of its public policy expenditures. "We use a balanced scorecard that has a lot of measurements in the public affairs area," explains Van Yeutter, director of Washington operations and international business relations for Cargill. He acknowledges that it's more difficult to quantify many of the important outcomes of public affairs expenditures, such as preventing government intervention, but he feels it's worth the effort. "It allows us to dialogue with governments about ideas, solutions, and depth of issues beyond what is just immediately important to Cargill," he explains. "I think that has developed trust in us that's appreciated by governments around the world."[32] In fact, Yeutter is surprised that more companies don't use the balanced scorecard in this way, since making the effort to quantify these outcomes makes it easier to justify them.

"My sense is that the more you see public affairs as a cost center, the less you will be involved in setting the agenda," Professor Schuler notes. He admires the Cargill effort to quantify the value of building political relationships. "Without these metrics, it's difficult to know the payoff."

It's also important to get ahead of the wave, especially if you are too small to set the agenda by yourself. By carefully monitoring the environment, you will know when government-sponsored changes are coming your way. Accepting the inevitable and moving ahead with solutions immediately will save money and headaches in the long run, especially if those solutions are more than minimally compliant.

Try also to meet or exceed the standards worldwide, being in synch with the strictest market requirements, whether legislated by governments or demanded by consumers. That way, in addition to avoiding barriers to entry in any market, your corporate reputation in even the strictest market will never be compromised. Many large companies that sell sophisticated equipment to an international clientele have learned this lesson well. Both Airbus and Boeing, for example, use the same quiet GE engine to meet or surpass tough European Union regulations limiting noise. These planes can be used without much danger of violating noise regulations anywhere in the world.[33]

Benefits can be had by taking action 180 degrees removed from your industry's image. Cement manufacturing is not widely known as a clean industry, but Cemex, a Mexico-based global cement company, has been quietly pursuing alternative fuels since 1991. The company's original goal was simply to reduce energy costs, which account for about 40 percent of its expenses. The first projects involved the clean burning of both tires and solvents, which had always been environmentally hazardous but could now be used as an energy source. "Not only do we get inexpensive fuel, but the companies that need to get rid of these things will pay us for destroying them," says Armando Garcia, Cemex executive vice president of development.[34] Not a bad business model—making money from pollution—but the company really hit on something when it persuaded the government of Mexico to fund a huge power plant fueled by petroleum coke (an oil refinery waste product, also called pet coke), which now supplies 60 percent of Cemex's energy needs in Mexico. The plant saves the company more than $120 million in fuel annually and consumes an environmental pollutant in the process.

Since Cemex began to burnish its reputation apart from the industry, the company's growth has approached 10 percent annually. "In the 1980s I realized that concentrating only on meeting the legal requirements of the countries in which we operated was not enough," says Garcia. "The bottom line is that our costs are manageable, and it gives us the recognition that we are leading the way." In 2002 Cemex was recognized by the World Environmental Center as "a model for Latin America and the world" with the Gold Medal for International Corporate Environmental Achievement.

Level the Playing Field

A company's reputation and trust with its stakeholders can be either helped or hurt to a significant degree by how well its leaders anticipate and respond to customer needs and sociopolitical realities. But engaging in the debate and turning risks into opportunities are only possible when there is a real commitment to creating enough trust among key influentials (especially governments) that will allow you to be heard—and believed.

Some companies assume they are not large or powerful enough to have a major impact on public policy in Washington or other capitals around the globe. At the 2006 World Economic Forum in Davos, CEOs stated in a survey that they believed that politicians only responded to pressure from people more powerful than themselves.[35] But you should never opt out of the game. You can have a major impact by working with officials who represent areas where you do business.

You don't have to lavish huge sums on either campaign contributions or lobbyists to be effective. Elected officials and regulators pay attention to constituencies, and to the experts. Building relationships with them—and impressing them with attention to your own stakeholders—is key to achieving a favorable outcome. Your experiences can make an important contribution to public discourse. Develop a finely tuned ear for actions that will not look self-serving, but are in fact in tune with corporate goals. Don't wait until you actually need something to gear up a response to actions in the public arena.

"For good or bad, a firm's marketplace strategy cannot be delinked from its public affairs and corporate political strategy," says Wake Forest management professor Michael Lord. "Yet many managers tend to be reactive toward public policy issues in general and in regard to grassroots concerns more specifically. They tend to treat public policy issues as a periodic nuisance rather than as an integral concern of their ongoing, long-term corporate strategy. Instead of being continually alert and involved in order to work early, proactively, and cooperatively to shape public policy in their favor, many firms react in a startled, negative fashion only *after* the warning bell is sounded, when political initiatives already are well under way and unfavorable momentum is formidable."[36] The trust you create in the political arena as Gerber did and as other companies do every day, could well stave off onerous regulation or less-than-scrupulous competition.

CHECKLIST FOR ENGAGING IN THE POLITICAL DEBATE

1. **Use political engagement strategically.** Pursue a consistent dialogue with policy makers and constituencies that impact your business.

2. **Establish a structure within the organization** that is linked to top management. Don't delegate monitoring issues and contacting political figures to layers down in the organization.

3. **Be bold in your policy platform.** Don't be afraid to take a position that is not directly in synch with your current business but that reflects public sentiment, changing markets, and your own values.

4. **Act early.** Getting involved at an early stage will allow you to contribute to shaping policies and help you to navigate any new regulatory paths.

5. **Don't underestimate your abilities.** Regardless of your company's size, you can have an effect on public policy. All companies with a passionate and sound position on an issue can significantly shape policy debate and social concerns.

6. **Don't dismiss an issue as too local.** In today's global environment, sociopolitical challenges in small markets can quickly catch fire and travel the world. Monitoring all engagements and watching competitor activity are crucial to retaining flexibility.

9

Respecting Culture in the Drive for Performance

Man cannot live without an enduring faith.

Franz Kafka[1]

There's tension here. We have to balance being a competitive leader and being a benevolent employer. But we have to be consistent with the heritage of Starbucks.

Howard Schultz
Chairman, Starbucks[2]

A LOT OF attention has been devoted to continual change as a critical element in enhancing performance in a global environment. But change of any kind is unsettling, and can be profoundly threatening to employees. A 2005 study of mergers and acquisitions by Boston College's Center for Corporate Responsibility found that about half of all mergers result in culture clashes, some of them extremely serious. "Usually you have the big company saying to the small one, 'You can pretty much run your own shop—except that we're cutting your costs, reviewing your marketing plan, and approving personnel decisions,'" says Phillip H. Mirvis, a coauthor of the study. "That sucks the life out of an organization."[3] It also shakes up company values and the way people are used to doing things.

The Boston College study provides increasing evidence that executives who do not pay sufficient heed to the culture are ripe for failure. Culture is not something you can take for granted or easily transform. But if you carefully and empirically analyze its strengths, and harness them judiciously, you can generate the kind of trust that will allow you to enact changes and build a more nimble and resilient company.

In my experience, few leaders pay enough attention to respecting and nurturing the cultures of the companies they lead through change, whether they are outsiders brought in to accomplish the transformation or insiders who should already be steeped in the culture. Both insiders and outsiders are, in fact, usually surprised by the depth of negative—or indifferent—reaction to their plans to move the company in a new direction. They shouldn't be. Departure from what people are comfortable with is likely to be fought passionately even when, rationally, such a change could be expected to be good for the company in the long run. Even a company with a committed leader who communicates well the need to set a new path may still face a great deal of resistance. This is particularly true in cases where an organization has fared well in the past, delivering consistently profitable results, but is no longer doing so in the present.

Probably the most publicized example in recent years of how difficult it is to bring change to an established organization is what happened to Carly Fiorina, the former head of Hewlett-Packard, who was fired in 2005 after losing the confidence of the board of directors. It was an ending Fiorina seemed almost to will on herself by her failure, in the eyes of employees, to sufficiently respect the "HP Way." In the end, whether "the HP way" was objectively an effective business model for the company's future mattered little. Fiorina doomed herself by paying too little attention to the fact that at the same time business practices are being transformed, the company's culture must be transformed as well. And of the two, transforming the culture is actually the much more difficult task. That's why the best leaders go out of their way to grow from old roots in order to enhance a new business model. To get on board, people need to see something familiar in the new strategy.

To achieve success, it is critical that management retain the trust of the company's employees even as the company changes. It is important that people identify with the values and new directions by seeing at least some of their heritage sustained. When Daniel Vasella merged Sandoz and Ciba-Geigy to form Novartis in 1996, he knew that success depended on forming a new company with a new identity and a new name. But he also emphasized that Novartis would take the best of both former companies, like a child that takes the best of both parents.

Respect for some of the old ways helps to ensure that there is real alignment around a new strategy and business focus, which is essential to building growth. There are many other examples besides Carly Fiorina at HP, of course. Motorola was another company in serious need of a shake-up when Ed Zander took over as CEO in January 2004. It consistently trailed competitors Nokia and Samsung Electronics and had a reputation of being inward-looking and somewhat sleepy. It was expected that Zander would replace the management team in the drive to achieve top performance. "What I heard," said Zander, "is that you have to come in and fire everyone and get your own team."[4] But he surprised observers by taking it slow, digging into the company's culture with extensive meetings and interviews with both employees and customers. Only then did he begin to move the company in a new direction, unlocking potential within the ranks and with existing leadership. "It was a seventy-five-year-old company with a history and culture and, before you go trigger-happy, there might be some gems here," he explained.[5]

A large body of international literature suggests that there is a strong, positive link between a corporation's culture, employee satisfaction, and its financial performance.[6] If corporate leaders can tap into the strengths of the company's culture, they will retain the trust and commitment of the workforce as change occurs. When they can count on the support of employees, they can much more easily ramp up other components of performance.

The trends that challenge the ability of leaders to move fast while preserving cultural roots include globalization, shaking a calcified company into performance mode, attempting to digest an acquisition (or resist being digested), or simply looking for novel paths to boost profitability. To achieve success, each of these changes demands leadership, alignment, and leveraging cultural strengths.

Globalizing a Culture at Starbucks

In 1971 Starbucks opened its first retail outlet in Seattle's colorful Pike Place Market, the nation's oldest continuously operating farmer's market, where today more than 9 million tourists a year are awed by the miles of produce and entertained by merchants slinging fresh fish overhead. At the start, however, Starbucks didn't even serve coffee by the cup, but merely sold the beans processed by its nearby coffee-roasting facility. In 1982 the marketing director, Howard Schultz, took a trip through Italy sipping espressos, and the thought occurred to him to serve premium coffee at his own stores cup by cup. When he couldn't convince the owners of Starbucks to buy into his idea, he left the company and tested the theory by opening a single coffee bar, Il Giornale, in downtown Seattle. Five years later he acquired the original Starbucks and became its chairman and began to lay the foundation for the hugely successful global juggernaut that Starbucks has become. Starbucks distinguished itself by selling premium coffee drinks prepared by friendly, intelligent, knowledgeable employees and thereby put into place the building blocks of a culture that keeps vast armies of modestly paid workers happy.[7]

"We recognized early on that the equity of the Starbucks brand was going to be the retail experience that the customers had in our stores," says Schultz. "There wasn't money for traditional advertising—and even if we'd had it, I don't think it would have been effective. So the investment we made was in creating a unique relationship with our people and getting them to understand that if the battle cry of the company was 'to exceed the expectations of our customers,' then as managers we had to first exceed the expectations of our people."[8]

In the Starbucks world, employees are called "partners." In order to attract the best applicants and keep them happy, the company provides anyone who works twenty hours or more per week a benefits package that includes health insurance, stock options, and a 401(k) plan with matching funds. Schultz calls these benefits "key components to our business model,"[9] and John Pence, professor of strategic management and entrepreneurship at Villanova University, agrees. He attributes the worldwide success of Starbucks to its culture-deep understanding of what makes the company successful. He points to Starbucks' worldwide policy of providing generous benefits, including a free pound of coffee beans every week, as incentive for "partners" to project a welcoming attitude toward customers. Starbucks spends more on health insurance, in fact, than on wholesale coffee beans. And in a training methodology unheard of in the rest of the convenience food industry, partners are typically flown into Seattle for eight intensive weeks of training and indoctrination into the Starbucks way.

This is the crux of creating a company that harnesses the power of trust. Corporate leaders must give their people a reason—or better yet, several reasons—to embrace the purpose of the company and in that way be empowered and motivated to establish good relationships with their customers. Actions needed to connect with customers—or innovate, or control costs, or produce error-free work—don't occur consistently unless they are built into the fabric of the culture.

Starbucks is relying on its partners around the world to fuel its ambitious expansion plans. The goal is to ramp up international growth in Europe, but especially in Asia, where China is the priority market, so that Starbucks will be within reach of most of the world's population by the end of this decade. The special relationship between partners and customers can also help to increase revenue by including a broader experience that includes entertainment, especially music and movies. Building on the core business model of the Starbucks experience, Schultz added CD sales in the stores, acquired the music retailer Hear Music, and added a twenty-four-hour music channel on XM Satellite Radio.

Starbucks' faith in its employees is rewarded by an annual employee turnover rate of less than half the industry average. This compares extremely favorable to the 200 percent turnover at most fast food chains and represents a vast savings for Starbucks in training and recruitment costs.[10] Internal surveys show that 87 percent of employees say they are "satisfied" or "very satisfied" with their jobs,[11] a sentiment that is communicated to the customer with their professionalism and commitment.

Starbucks clearly expects to leverage its unique culture, recognizing that there is still plenty of opportunity for growth, both in the United States and elsewhere. Even with all its success, Starbucks still accounts for less than 10 percent of the total coffee consumed in North America.[12] In order to continue to strengthen the Starbucks brand, the company is seeking to enlarge the Starbucks experience, banking on a new phrase, "the Starbucks Effect." The concept refers to the impact Starbucks has on partners, customers, and communities around the world. "The Starbucks Effect embodies the very essence of the Starbuck culture," says Schultz. "We recognize the relationship between the success of our company and the strength and vitality of all communities in which we operate. And it all begins with a cup of coffee."[13]

The purpose of emphasizing the Starbucks Effect is not to diverge from the coffee business, but to continue to increase shareholder value and open new growth potential by reinforcing the brand's possibilities to deliver the "human connection." One question is whether Starbucks can retain its differentiated culture as it embarks on a plan to get most of its future growth outside the United States. Its goal is to open at least 15,000 additional stores overseas,[14] many of them in areas of great cultural diversity. About 50 stores were opened in China in 2005, bringing the total there to

221. Schultz himself spent an increasing amount of time in China, meeting partners both in the company's operated and licensed stores. In 2005 Starbucks was recognized as one of the top ten employers in China by CCTV, the national television network.[15]

Pedro Man, president of Starbucks Coffee in the Asia-Pacific region, already oversees more than 1,100 outlets in Asia. He believes it will be particularly vital to make a connection with customers in countries where people may not be very familiar with coffee and where tea is the much-preferred hot drink. "It's a major point of differentiation between us and any other coffee supplier," says Man. "If we pass the knowledge to our customers, they will become brand ambassadors."

To ensure that employees can indeed pass on that knowledge, Man requires all Starbucks employees in Asia to complete a thirteen-week training program, including time in a coffee "aroma lab." Staff members hold weekly coffee socials among themselves, and the best employees are encouraged to compete against each other in a "coffee master program," a sort of coffee Olympics. Man is also committed to adhering to the other reinforcing factors of the Starbucks culture, including wages and fringe benefits that exceed the industry standard.[16]

Thus far, Starbucks has succeeded on the global stage by exporting its American culture wholesale to new outlets and employees. Starbucks top management believes that international employees want the same things American workers do: to have a decent reward for their work that goes beyond even money. "We're not giving these benefits because we're a successful company," says current Starbucks CEO Jim Donald. "We're successful because we're giving to our people."[17]

Culture as a Reason to Believe

Starbucks has created a culture that, so far at least, has proven resilient, even amid rocketing growth and intensifying competition. It seems to be exportable, as the company expands deep into China while continuing its growth in Japan, Korea, and Europe. It has proven to be a successful strategy because its leaders have persistently reinforced and exploited the true nature of its organizational culture.

As Starbucks continues to grow globally at breakneck speed, opening about five stores a day,[18] it will be putting to the test the idea that companies can be financially successful with a corporate culture that cares about its employees, customers, and the communities in which they operate. Many companies have gone the other way, squeezing profits from cost cutting and outsourcing. Providing employees health insurance and other benefits, maintaining stores with facilities like wireless access and a comfortable environment, and paying above market prices to third world coffee growers are all values that could be strained if there is an urgent need to improve profits. But Schultz is committed to the way the company does business.

"We have to balance being competitive leaders and being a benevolent employer," says Schultz, recognizing that these threats touch on the fundamental tenets of the Starbucks culture. "There's tension here, and I'm just trying to respond in a responsible way.[19]

A strong culture provides people with a reason to believe. One reason leaders brought in to accomplish radical change often fail, is that they believe that by setting a charismatic and strong example at the top, they give employees a role model they will want to follow. In the era of the hero leader, this was widely believed as gospel. In reality, it's not enough. Setting the stage for culture change by setting an example at the top is only the first, most basic step toward change.

Especially in an established company, the "way things are done around here" is a blending of past leadership and long-forgotten incidents that have become a part of the company's DNA. Trace a characteristic corporate behavior back as far as you can, and often even the longest-serving employee may have no idea why it "feels right" to proceed in a particular way. Leaders must understand that the "old ways" will persist beyond all reason and must be consciously channeled into new paths. The leader's role in changing culture must, therefore, proceed from the obvious to the hidden, from what is seen to what can only be surmised.

The Status Quo Is Not Enough

It's important to communicate any cultural change, no matter how seemingly insignificant. That will mean creating an understandable model of what you want to accomplish. If you wish your people to share ideas across functions, you must be willing to consider radical departures from the status quo at all levels of the company. If you want people to embrace "lean manufacturing," for example, you must lose any vestiges of an entourage or status symbols that may be difficult to jettison. Employees won't look for every nickel of savings if they see their leaders wasting even a penny. In order to model effectively, leaders must be completely clear in their own mind about their cultural strategy, and must be prepared to defend it. While it obviously makes sense to study the culture of a company to be acquired in detail, in any situation of cultural change you must clearly formulate a "target culture" before you can hope to see it develop.

Even as you strenuously make the case for change, don't expect that change to occur quickly. Employees must understand the need for culture change intellectually before they will make a single move in that direction. It will likely take more time and effort than you anticipate, but don't let that fact discourage you from persistently communicating your message.

The process of change will make it acceptable to question everything. Cultural biases only become visible once they are acknowledged. Unspoken assumptions most often develop into cultural conflicts when you are attempting to lead teams that may be widely dispersed around the globe—or even in disparate areas of the same country. Virtual technology has made such teams more likely to develop, and more productive when they do. But it has also made it more difficult for such teams to succeed without an effort by leaders to help them understand both their differences and common ground.

Research by British consultant Chris Speechley shows that differences in national culture among team members do not matter as much as "disparities in organizational culture, across sites, disciplines and functions." As a result, Speechley believes that command-and-control systems will be ineffective in managing cross-cultural or cross-functional teams, and that inclusion and trust are the leadership qualities that most effectively defuse cultural conflict.[20]

It will also be important to develop an ownership mind-set about culture change. Steps specifically intended to incentivize employees toward driving the change already underway at the top may include enlisting their help in leading "change workshops" or measuring their own capacity for change. They may also include less subtle measures, like tying compensation or bonuses directly to their participation in change-inducing behavior or activities. Leaders will find themselves on shaky ground if they try to impose a culture from on high by training people to "accept" the new ways. Far better to charge employees with the task of changing each other to meet the challenges of global competition. For isn't culture nothing more than each company's evolved method of working with its stakeholders? One of the Merriam-Webster Dictionary's definitions of "culture" is "the integrated pattern of human knowledge, belief, and behavior that depends upon man's capacity for learning and transmitting knowledge to succeeding generations." Substitute "stakeholders" for "succeeding generations" and a rationale for corporate behavior emerges.

Performance-Based Culture Change

Changing a culture and coming out on the other side with a successfully performing company will require patience. Swift, radical change rarely produces a resilient culture. Companies that move too quickly must be prepared for cultural upheavals that may derail much of the intended benefit. Even massive layoffs rarely shift the underlying cultural norms of a company.

In a world that demands nimble companies willing to change quickly, it is a challenge to make certain that change is accomplished in a timely manner without getting bogged down in endless arguments over goals and tactics. Nitin Nohria, the Richard P. Chapman Professor of Business Administration at Harvard University, suggests creating a top-to-bottom performance culture, with specific rewards for meeting specific goals. In a multiyear study of the best practices within more than 160 major companies, Nohria found that the companies that did the best had cultures most attuned to rewarding those who met goals. In fact, at the highest-performing companies, "no bonuses, stock options or other rewards were given when targets were missed. These organizations design and support a culture that encourages outstanding individual and team contributions, one that holds employees—not just managers—responsible for success."[21]

Nohria discovered that at the highest-performing companies, goals like on-time performance, quality, and logistics were just as important as improving financial numbers—and as intimately tied to competitive success. Nohria singles out steelmaker Nucor as an example of a winning company truly committed to its performance-based culture. During the period Nohria and his team studied (1986–1996), Nucor consistently outperformed its competitors, yet its officers earned lower salaries than they could have at competing companies and had "no employment contracts, retirement programs or annuities." Their bonuses depended entirely on increases in annual return on stockholder's equity. This is very far from the current fashion, which holds that, in order to win employee loyalty, especially from young people, companies must provide not only high salaries, but opportunities for fun at work. Nohria's research demonstrates that the fun is in the achievement.

Too Much, Too Fast: Carly Fiorina and Hewlett-Packard

In the end Carly Fiorina lost her job as CEO of Hewlett-Packard because the company consistently fell short of its financial performance goals. She had other problems too, however, more related to culture than performance. That's because there are many reasons, some performance and some culture related. Certainly her troubles mounted with the acrimonious opposition, led by the company's largest shareholder, Walter Hewlett, heir to one of HP's founders, to the $18.7 billion acquisition of Compaq. By battling the son of founder Bill Hewlett, Fiorina was symbolically challenging HP traditions. She labored hard to sell the merger to shareholders with a proxy battle that lasted more than six months. She argued that the merger was essential to strengthening the company's competitive standing in hardware by becoming a full-service technology company, and expanding beyond the company's core business of printers. It was hoped, by both Fiorina and HP's board, that doing so would provide a great advantage against rivals IBM and Dell. But at the time of the merger, the desktop personal computer had already become almost a commodity, something IBM finally acknowledged two years later when it unloaded its PC business to low-cost Chinese producer Lenovo. Many critics at the time saw the merger as a case of two wrongs not making a right, calling it "Fiorina's Folly."[22]

Opposing the Hewlett family was symbolic. Fiorina was not taking into account the strong, independent cultural traditions that had always driven HP, famously started by "two guys in a garage," Bill Hewlett and his Stanford University classmate Dave Packard. The two engineers began in 1939 by making oscillators, but by the time the company went public in 1957, their product had expanded into a full line of testing and measuring equipment. Along the way Hewlett and Packard had developed the set of management principles that would become known as "the HP Way." It was a culture that valued respect, collaboration, entrepreneurial effort, individual contribution, and passion for customers—a culture, in other words, that was built for engineers. Fiorina was brought in to break the mold and drive a more vigorous marketing mind-set into the company in order to win in a fast-changing, fiercely competitive industry. Many argued that in order to be successful in the increasingly difficult market, changes to HP's softer, more team-building culture were needed.

By the mid-1970s HP was known for its powerful calculators and had begun its move into business computing. During this same time, it became the first U.S. company to introduce such workplace innovations as flextime, whereby employees could vary their start and stop times as long as they worked the required eight hours a day.

It was the kind of family-friendly move that by the 1980s would win it the deep loyalty and trust of HP employees, particularly women.[23] HP was extremely late to capitalize on the technology boom. It continued to emphasize incremental change, although the marketplace was demanding a very different business model.

Fiorina was hired to shake things up, and she immediately took steps to inject a new sense of urgency into HP. To create a focused market-driven organization, Fiorina reorganized HP's eighty operating units into four key groups, all centered on customers, speed, and aggressive sales targets. She centralized branding and advertising, and in 2001, she dismissed about 7 percent of the workforce, at that time the largest layoff in HP history. This was a shock for a company that had historically adhered to an employment-for-life philosophy. But for a salesperson like Fiorina, it made perfect sense: If you wanted to be competitive and increase revenue, you had to create a new mind-set and attack the "cultural inertia" that was preventing more sales from being made.[24] One of her biggest successes, for example, was HP's winning a $3 billion ten-year contract to provide Procter & Gamble with IT services. HP beat out IBM, among others, because "they were very focused and they were very, very hungry," according to Andrew Hewat of Texas-based TPI, lead consultant to P&G on the deal. IBM was reportedly stunned when it heard HP had won the contract.[25]

In the process, however, Fiorina was ignoring the needs of HP engineers, the company's historic focus. In fact, to many insiders she was perceived as seemingly unwilling to capitalize on any positive forces that might have made employees—or the board—more loyal to her. She broke with tradition, for example, by only rarely eating or mingling with employees. And although she told business students at Toronto's York University, "Everything is possible at HP," in the same speech she implied that many of those who worked at HP were focused on the wrong priorities. "One of the things that I remind both customers and employees of HP is that technology is not an end in itself, although sometimes technologists fall in love with the technology," she said.[26]

But falling in love with technology—or whatever your company does best—is the way to build a culture that is strong enough to support other needed changes. And that support is what will allow leaders to keep their job long enough to get the job done.

As Fiorina headed into her third year at the helm of HP, the company's performance continued to lag. Profit targets were frequently missed, and the promises made in the merger proxy statement, especially regarding margin improvement, were not being kept.

The exodus of talent didn't help, either. In August 2004, in the wake of yet another missed quarter of profit forecasts, Fiorina publicly fired three senior sales executives, blaming them for the shortfall. This triggered yet another wave of recognition that things were continuing to deteriorate.

Perhaps Carly Fiorina could have sustained the confidence of her employees and the board of directors and would still be at the helm of HP if she had paid sufficient attention to attuning her personal style to the culture she was trying to steer into more profitable avenues. Former HP CEO Lew Platt, who had hired Fiorina as his successor, believed "she would be a terrific change agent" and exactly what the company needed to blast its culture into the new century. But, like the board of directors, he came to realize there was a critical flaw in her strategy. "We also thought she would be more closely aligned with the HP culture than she actually is," said Platt a few years later.

Fiorina's style struck a "rock star celebrity" note, diverging far from the HP culture, which had been defined by open doors, top management mingling with employees, and casual dress. In contrast, Fiorina rarely ate in the company cafeteria, and she maintained an aggressive travel schedule that made it difficult for employees to get a face-to-face meeting with her. She sought to wow her employees with large, staged town hall meetings, PowerPoint slides, and the entertainment glitz of light shows and celebrities such as Magic Johnson. She increased the number of corporate jets and drew personal criticism for her autocratic management style, coiffed hairstyles, and fashion-plate attire. For a company that had prided itself on modesty, Fiorina's appearance in the company corporate ads, launched at the end of 1999, looked like self-promotion. Comments on the company intranet were so hostile and critical that the page, which was set up to receive employee responses, was eventually shut down.[27]

Stresses from the merger and the fierce market competition certainly contributed to tension among employees, but in the end Fiorina's "superstar status" was her undoing.[28] Her high visibility, marketing-driven style gave rise to a bitter divide between passionate supporters and bitter enemies, but she couldn't overcome the internal resentment over her belief that the HP Way was, as *Wall Street Journal* reporter Michael Malone put it, "mystical, managerial mumbo-jumbo that was obsolete thirty years ago."[29]

Fiorina's change plan was probably too radical and too quick. The backlash forced her to slow down.[30] There was also insufficient attention to what could and could not be changed. Earnings were far below analysts' expectations in the third quarter of 2004. In the end, lack of performance essentially sealed Fiorina's fate. It also didn't help that HP's share price had declined more than 50 percent since she became CEO in July 1999.

When Fiorina was dismissed in February 2005, many observers believed her firing was simply a matter of Fiorina being unable to run the business properly or to design and execute good strategies.[31] But Fiorina was ultimately fired because she lost the trust of many of her employees and the confidence of her most critical stakeholder group, the HP board of directors. Robert P. Wayman, who took over for Fiorina on an interim basis while a search for her successor was under way, revealed the board's thinking when he promised flatly that the new CEO would be "someone who will fit with the culture."[32]

Fiorina's situation is a clear example of what can happen when there is a serious misalignment between a change agent and the culture that agent was brought in to change. At first, employees were shocked by her sudden departure, but then e-mails began circulating expressing a collective sigh of relief. Supposedly, on the day of her departure someone played "Ding Dong! The Witch Is Dead" on internal loudspeakers. More telling was that the stock price rose 6.9 percent on the news that Fiorina had been forced out.

Mark Hurd, hired as the new CEO to replace Fiorina, is her antithesis. Quiet and unassuming, he is actually shy of press attention. More important, he hopes to get the company back on track by bringing things more in line with the HP way. He says he will seek to "combine simple objectives, enlightened business practices, trust in employees and ruthless self-appraisal to make the right choices." In fact, as illustrated below, HP shares have dramatically recovered since Hurd took over.

Hewlett-Packard–Mark Hurd Named CEO

Three-year daily stock performance for Hewlett-Packard

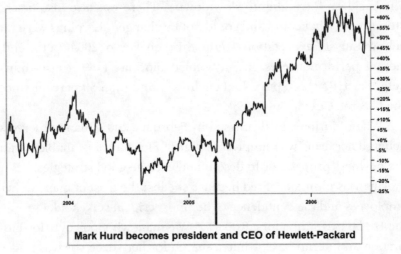

Mark Hurd becomes president and CEO of Hewlett-Packard

Go Slow, Capitalize on Strengths

Fiorina probably didn't do anything wrong. In fact, she attempted to do what her board wanted her to do: transform a stodgy, engineering-focused company into a nimble, marketing-focused one. The fact that she tried to do this incredibly fast and through the instrument of a merger merely compounded the problems. Any executive who tries to change a culture faces them. In a four-year study of major European companies, British author and former McKinsey & Company consultant George Binney found that transforming business culture is much harder than most leaders—and even more important, most boards of directors—expect. "We found that leaders could not transform their business environment, organizational culture and people, and group dynamics in the way they hoped," he writes. "All but one of the leaders studied set out to achieve a complete change—a business turnaround, a fundamental change of culture, or the development of a new enterprise. Try as they would to wrench their organizations into submission, their organizations bit back."

Binney notes that the leaders he studied were not considered failures and were not, typically, dismissed for failing to achieve the cultural transformations they set out to put in place. Rather, they improved their environment in small increments, and as a single organization tried to achieve a common goal. "We saw in our research that it was the quality of relationships that leaders and groups established which delivered results," he concludes. "People work for people—not for visions or strategies or targets—and give their best when they feel connected to the leader and the leader feels connected to them."[33]

In HP's case, new CEO Mark Hurd is attempting to capitalize on the engineering-oriented strengths in the company's culture, while at the same time implementing strict financial controls. He does not believe that leaders can "inspire" changes in the culture, "I think you have to give people more of a process than that," he says. "You have to give them clarity of objectives, tell them 'I expect you to do this; I expect you to deliver what you've committed to.'"[34]

At the same time, Hurd seems to realize the importance of tapping into the collective pride that HP has always had in the HP Way, which in the past inspired innovation. Very soon after he took the helm he pledged to do "everything in his power" to live up to Hewlett's and Packard's dedication to the search for innovation.[35]

But Hurd knows that HP must do more than simply go back to

the past. He believes that financial metrics are at least as important as culture, but that neither should dominate. As he writes in his book *The Value Factor*, "To manage effectively in today's information-driven market environment, executives must create a corporate culture in which creativity and the ability to manage change are fostered without losing control over core operations."[36] That sounds like a good fit with the HP Way, and could very well help the company regain its equilibrium.

Acquiring a Culture

Just as young people learn when they first start out in their careers that it pays to be alert for clues to whether they will be a fit with the company where they are interviewing, leaders, too, have to pay attention to the culture they are inheriting. The culture will always fight back if the changes demanded are deemed too great. Only by capitalizing on the culture at the same time changes are made will it be possible to remold a company into something even stronger than before.

That's exactly what happened when Unilever took over the Ben & Jerry's ice cream company in 2001. Unilever could have forced the tiny company to toe the corporate line, given that Ben & Jerry's 520 employees were no more than a blip in Unilever's 230,000-strong workforce. But Unilever chairman Antony Burgmans wisely avoided altering what had made the company what it was: a brand identified with progressive causes, caring people, and a humorous, irreverent way of looking at ice cream sales and flavors. He and new CEO Yves Couette, a Unilever veteran, decided instead to fix what needed fixing—what even people inside Ben & Jerry's could agree needed improvement. An internal survey showed that only 29 percent of Ben & Jerry's employees thought the business side of things was running properly. Only half thought their bosses were good at planning for the future.[37] With everything else they wanted to leave well enough alone.

To communicate his support for the Ben & Jerry's culture, Couette abandoned his usual business suit and came to the office as casually dressed as his employees. Because internal surveys showed that commitment to Ben & Jerry's social mission was important to most of those who worked there, he also participated in community activities supported by the company. But Couette's most critical decision was probably to encourage Ben & Jerry's employees to decide for themselves which Unilever programs, if adopted at Ben & Jerry's, would improve performance. An informal group, made up of company leaders from marketing, finance, human resources, and public relations, was established to mimic Ben & Jerry's tradition of hallway meetings. A company-wide contest even came up with a name for the new committee—Managers of Mission, or Mom.

As a result of these and other moves to retain or improve the existing culture, Unilever has been able to preserve a valued part of the goodwill it purchased in the quirky soul of Ben & Jerry's. It has also allowed employees to retain the social values so important to many of them. Even better, this cultural sensitivity has helped Ben & Jerry's to grow very nicely. Between 2001 and 2004 it increased global sales by 37 percent, boosted operating margins by 300 percent, and expanded into thirteen countries.[38]

Daimler-Benz is another example of an acquiring company which recognized, eventually, the need to allow its American subsidiary to play to its strengths. In Chrysler's case, these were strengths that had taken a generation to develop. Founded in 1925 by Walter Percy Chrysler, the company had fostered an environment in which employees were expected to follow orders. Engineers and managers were almost gods; their word was law. Unfortunately, sales kept declining as customers grew increasingly dissatisfied with the quality of the cars Chrysler manufactured.

But in the years prior to the merger with Daimler-Benz, Chrysler launched an intensive effort to improve quality. Line workers were retrained to question anything that might impact safety, productivity, or quality, even if it meant shutting down the line to fix a problem. For the first time, employees were given access to senior managers and engineers and expected to help solve problems. Employees began to understand that their opinions were valued.

After the acquisition was made final, Daimler's mainly German executive team was surprised at the depth of commitment to questioning management's judgment, an approach that was not particularly valued within its own culture. Wisely, Daimler not only left Chrysler's new culture alone, but it brought in new systems to take advantage of it. Chrysler's new lean manufacturing initiative, for example, which includes recognition for all employee efforts to streamline work processes, is now being expanded to every plant and facility.[39]

Some mergers, of course, struggle for years to mesh two very different cultures. Sony chairman Nobuyuki Idei, speaking from the experience of his company's acquisition of MGM/United Artists, counsels patience when taking on the challenge. "It took nearly ten years since we acquired the different culture [movie studio] before we started talking positively to each other," he says.[40]

When Steve Case and Gerald M. Levin orchestrated the blockbuster merger in 2000 of Time Warner and AOL, they knew there would be problems because the organizations had such different values. At the outset they insisted that they were working "carefully to strike a reasonable compromise on the values of their two companies." At the time the deal seemed to make sense as a union of strengths, merging the world's largest entertainment company with the most successful brand name on the Internet. For AOL, it represented an opportunity to access a broadband network to replace its dial-up business model. Time Warner, in turn, wanted to add AOL's 20 million Internet subscribers to its portfolio of entertainment outlets. "This is a perfect fit," Steve Case claimed. "No company will be better equipped to capitalize on the convergence of media, entertainment and communications."[41]

But Case and Levin should have looked more closely at the symbolism on display the day the merger was announced. Case's tie and business suit and Levin's open collar were intended to demonstrate the unification of two very different companies. Instead, it offered a clue that the merger would be fraught with cultural conflicts between the buttoned-down Time Warner and the rolled-up-sleeved

AOL. Certainly AOL and Time Warner should have more carefully considered whether they really belonged together. The expensive venture, burdening the new company with debt, is generally considered to be one of the most spectacularly ill-advised corporate mergers in U.S. history.

Still, the surviving company has managed to make the best of the situation. In 2002 Wharton marketing professor Joshua Eliashberg predicted, "AOL Time Warner is clearly not going to survive. You can't decide to acquire another business if it's only remotely related to your core competency."[42] That clearly hasn't happened. Although Time Warner did not, in fact, give AOL access to broadband as was originally envisioned, once Internet advertising rebounded from its spectacular crash, AOL did finally begin to contribute to Time Warner's profitability in a meaningful way. In fact, although the company's stock price continues to languish, its earnings since the dot-com crash of 2002 have actually been the second highest in the diversified entertainment segment, trailing only Disney, and not by much.[43] Not bad for a company whose merger almost knocked it out for good. Somehow its leaders have managed to cobble together a workable culture, though trial and error and a lot of communications between the two groups.

Reliable Predictors of Culture Change

All companies, because they must be responsive to the marketplace, should expect shifts in their cultural underpinnings. But leaders need to know how to successfully manage culture shifts, while at the same time maintaining the fundamentals as the market changes and as new trends emerge. There are notable common characteristics shared by companies that have navigated these changes, but in my experience there are also certain guidelines most companies overlook while trying to achieve growth in ways that can test the mettle of the company's cultural traditions.

Leaders have a relatively easy task when all they have to do is capitalize on the strengths of an existing culture. A much more significant challenge is posed when an organization's very survival depends on making wrenching changes in the norms and priorities under which the company has always operated. Even in these instances, retaining some values of the company's culture helps build alignment. After the 2003 crash of the shuttle *Columbia,* the National Aeronautics and Space Administration (NASA) realized they had to change a culture in which the people at the top were exceptionally unwilling to listen to bad news. A survey of NASA employees by Behavioral Science Technology, Inc., of Ojai, California, showed that "safety is something to which NASA personnel are strongly committed in concept, but NASA has not reflected the values it prizes most." It found that problems were not being communicated upward because of fear that careers could be stalled for reporting something that might reflect badly on NASA. Respecting NASA's mission-driven culture enabled the agency to break the dysfunctional barriers that were preventing a strong communications flow up and down the line. NASA embarked on a program that included one-on-one coaching, 360-degree performance evaluations, and data-driven interventions to spot organizational barriers. Progress was made because everyone felt they were part of a shared purpose, not fighting against values embedded in the culture.

Employees will work harder when they see that their leaders believe in them. That's the only way to be sure they will execute programs designed to move the organization closer to new markets or emerging customer needs. Companies that invest in their people will likely see a greater increase in productivity. In a 2003 study of three thousand companies, researchers at the University of Pennsylvania found that capital improvements add about 4 percent to productivity, while similar investments in human capital added more than twice that much.[44] Why, indeed, should employees who feel undervalued by their company ever go out of their way to stretch themselves and adapt to change? Only when employees feel important and valued will they create in customer's minds what Jan Carlzon, the former CEO of Scandinavian Airlines calls "moments of truth." He brought the airline back from the brink of bankruptcy by convincing employees that every ten-second interaction with a customer was an opportunity to create a moment of truth. In the millions of those moments every day was a chance to "create a favorable impression a million times a day, one moment at a time."[45]

By communicating new mind-sets and new behaviors, leaders of every organization have the opportunity to create those moments of truth, both in their personal interactions and with the policy actions that affect people throughout the corporation. Employees must understand the need for culture change intellectually before they will make a single move in that direction. If you wish your people to share ideas across functions, you must be willing to experiment with—or at least listen to—radical departures from the status quo at all levels of the company. Creating effective mass communication avenues that connect consistently and repeatedly with employees and customers—and always conveying an understanding of their needs—is vital.

It is important to be on the lookout for cultural disparities. Studies show that in France, for example, leaders tend to value their autonomy. Two-thirds of French corporate leaders cite "the freedom to make a decision with minimum interference" as one of the best things about their job, compared to 39 percent in the United Kingdom. Seventy percent of British leaders rate "developing talent in the company" as one the best things about their job, compared to 14 percent in France.[46] These differences act as a screen, which can often distort messages and lead to mistaken assumptions, especially when so much of communications today is virtual.

At many successful companies, the culture is tailored to encourage specific outcomes. At Apple Computer, employees are permitted to come to work in a dress if they want—even if they're male.[47] What better signal that the company values out-of-the-box, no-holds-barred thinking? It's also a message that has somehow translated into blockbuster consumer products, most recently inspiring the iPod phenomenon, an entirely new way to experience music.

Another company that has created a stable yet innovative culture is the computer company Dell. To ensure that his executives continue to look for new ideas, founder Michael Dell splits business units in half when they get to a certain size. He believes that leaders who stay focused on a very small piece of the puzzle are more likely to recognize innovations with potential. According to Michael Treacy, cofounder of Dell subsidiary GEN3 Partners, this "narrows the focus of each executive so that he or she can go to a much deeper level of innovation."[48] In this way Dell neatly avoids the problem of "bigness" that plagues so many enterprises as they grow.

A burgeoning bureaucracy tends to feed itself, growing exponentially as more and more people need to be supervised. With a heightened need for rules comes a lowering of incentives for innovation. Regardless of the size of the company or business unit, leaders need to make certain that the culture is one with which people can identify and align, and yet is structured to reinforce the business goals they are trying to encourage.

CHECKLIST FOR RESPECTING CULTURE THROUGH TRANSFORMATIONAL CHANGE

1. **Embrace the organization's purpose.** To excel and achieve a sustained competitive position, people need a reason to believe and companies need a purpose. This must be embedded in the values and tenets of the company's culture.

2. **Make the case for change.** When market forces, competition, and customer demands drive the need for change, carefully explain what's happening. People need to intellectually understand the imperative to move to a new vision and way of doing business before they will get behind the changes taking place.

3. **Build on the traditions.** To help employees identify with where you want to take the organization, respect the culture, and build on it, while creating something new.

4. **Meet face to face.** Cultural evolutions are difficult. Communicate repeatedly and in person. In large multinational organizations, national differences can distort the way a message is received because people will have different expectations, attitudes toward authority, methods of team interaction, and ways of leading. Disparities across sites can be as great as variations in different functions and disciplines. Scientists think differently than marketing personnel. Regular in-person communications, complemented by e-mail, telephone, and video conferencing, can mitigate these differences.

5. **Test the capacity for change.** Understand your organization's capacity for change. How much, how fast, and in which parts of the company can it be accomplished? Don't just try to push down directives from the top. Put out the new vision and let people work together to uncover new and better behaviors within the boundaries that have been established.

6. **Be patient.** It will likely take more time and effort than you anticipate, but don't be discouraged. It takes time to create something valuable.

Conclusion

The Trust Imperative: A New Leadership Code

Companies don't understand that the level of scrutiny they are exposed to has escalated.

Michael Porter
Professor, Harvard Business School[1]

No one at Sun wants us to be just a great company with great technology. We also want Sun to be a good company—we believe we can change the planet.

Jonathan Schwartz
CEO, Sun Microsystems[2]

LET US HOPE the guilty verdicts in the Enron case marked the end of a period of over-the-top management excesses and moral failures. If so, it's just in time. Survey after survey demonstrates a declining trust in business. A January 2006 study by Opinion Research Corporation of Princeton, N.J., of adult investors in the United States found that only 39 percent of investors are confident that CEOs practice ethical business behavior, down from 47 percent a year earlier.

I believe we are entering a new corporate age in which trust can replace perceptions of dishonesty. This will happen if people are given reason to believe that corporate greed is giving way to corporate responsibility. It will take concerted efforts by business leaders to change the corporate landscape. Only then will we begin to see an opinion shift among the public.

Today's information environment makes the challenge only more difficult. News spreads quickly across the globe. In years past, small legal infractions or ethical lapses might have flown under the radar. Today there is nowhere to hide. As Thomas Dougherty of the Skadden Arps law firm puts it, "Instant communications has transformed individuals into interest groups and interest groups into Internet pressure groups."[3] As a result, corporate leaders who want to lead their companies to success need to focus on the trust imperative. That means recognizing that every stakeholder group is judging you every day. Only by making decisions based on personal and corporate values can you hope to gain public trust and cooperation.

This trust imperative is a code of leadership, consisting of both personal values and concrete action. It can be synthesized into eight clearly defined steps:

1. Define your personal leadership brand and communicate your values throughout the organization. Be accountable toward fulfilling them yourself, and make clear your expectations of others.

2. Be forthright to your stakeholders, particularly when there are problems, even if it means saying things you wish you didn't have to say. Don't overpromise; resist the temptation to paint a rosy picture. Make certain your statements are frank and that you set realistic expectations. Be honest, open, and transparent. Above all, be honest with yourself, which means telling yourself the hard truth at the same time you're telling it to others.

3. Listen twice as much as you speak—to employees, customers, and critics. You can learn from their different perspectives and be certain you have access to what is truly going on in the organization.

4. Ramp up your commitment to good corporate governance, including regulatory compliance, board independence, and shareholder outreach. Demonstrate to investors that you are prepared to go beyond regulations imposed by Sarbanes-Oxley and other new legislation.

5. Embrace your responsibilities to the communities where your company has a presence, and to those in need whom your company has a special responsibility to assist.

6. Engage policy makers and use your experience, knowledge, and commitment to shape the debate.

7. Build partnerships within your industry. Your company can't be expected to be experts in everything, but it can build on the experience of others.

8. Respect the roots of your culture. Even when making a sharp turn away from the business priorities of the past, retaining fundamental, deep-seated values can be a vital ingredient of success.

Not every successful corporate leader will follow each of these imperatives perfectly, and certainly most will not fulfill them correctly all of the time. There are certainly successful people profiled in the preceding pages who have done some of them well, but others poorly. Yet together these imperatives of trust add up to a new portfolio of responsibilities that can lead to a new, trustful age of corporate leadership. Some businessmen stand out for their ability to set high ethical and performance standards and realize them. For every businessperson derided in the press for their excesses, there are others, who may not get as much media attention, who show restraint and responsibility.

Leaders who follow the trust imperatives do so not to be well liked, receive personal credit, or even to stay out of jail. They do it because gaining the trust of stakeholders is becoming ever more critical to building a profitable business. According to Wharton School professor Thomas Donaldson, "Empirical studies have demonstrated that companies with good ethical reputations attract and retain better employees, that customers and suppliers are drawn to companies with better reputations for integrity, and that employees are more loyal to their company when they have a good impression of its ethics." Donaldson points to "massive literature" developed over the past two decades "detailing how, in many forms of business interactions, a failure of trust implies a loss in profits and benefits for everyone."[4]

The new climate in which business people operate demands a new code of leadership, one which requires considering the top job differently. To be successful, business leaders will need to take on a far broader portfolio of responsibilities. As trust becomes the new watchword of thriving leadership, those who adopt this new perspective, who follow the trust imperative in everything they do, will have a much better chance to achieve their goals of personal success and corporate performance.

Notes

1: Trusted Leadership as an Imperative for Success

1. Winston S. Churchill, Commencement Address at Harvard University, 1943.
2. U.S. Gallup poll, November 2004, http://www.gallup.com/.
3. Corporate Social Responsibility Monitor, GlobeScan, Inc., November 2003–February 2004.
4. Chuck Lucier, Rob Schuyt, and Eric Spiegel, "2002: Deliver or Depart," Booz Allen Hamilton's annual CEO Succession Study of the world's 2,500 largest public companies.
5. "CEO Turnover and Job Security—Research Highlights from a Worldwide Survey," Study sponsored by Drake, Beam & Morin, 2000.
6. Carol Hymowitz, "Still to Come . . . More CEOs on the Griddle . . . ," *Wall Street Journal*, December 31, 2005; Steven Hall & Partners, LLC, "Sixteen Percent CEO Turnover at Top Companies in 2005," http://www.shallpartners.com/pdfs/pr07Feb06.pdf.
7. "CEO Turnover and Job Security—Research Highlights from a Worldwide Survey," Study sponsored by Drake, Beam & Morin, 2000.
8. Arthur Levitt Jr., "The Imperial CEO Is No More," *Wall Street Journal*, March 17, 2005.
9. Chuck Lucier, Rob Schuyt, and Edward Tse, "CEO Succession 2004: The World's Most Prominent Temp Workers," Booz Allen Hamilton's annual CEO Succession Study of the world's 2,500 largest public companies.
10. Daniel Vasella, in discussion with the author, August 2005.
11. Daniel Vasella and Clifton Leaf, "Temptation Is All Around Us," *Fortune*, November 18, 2002.
12. Glenn Renwick, in discussion with Nancy Shepherdson, May 2005.
13. Joseph B. White and Stephen Power, "VW Chief Confronts Corporate

Culture—Pischetsrieder Says Too Little Customer Focus Is Auto Maker's Biggest Problem," *Wall Street Journal,* September 19, 2005.

14. Arthur Sulzberger Jr., in discussion with the author, June 2005.

15. Securities and Exchange Commission, SEC Annual Reports [2000-2004], http://www.sec.gov/about/secpar2005.shtml.

16. Patricia Callahan, Delroy Alexander, and Jeremy Manier, "As Fat Fears Grow, Oreo Tries New Twist, *Chicago Tribune,* August 22, 2005.

17. Ibid.

18. National Center for Charitable Statistics.

19. Novartis, for example, lacking a distribution system for its medicines in Africa, partnered with the World Health Organization to get the medicines where they were needed.

2: Profitable Responsibility

1. The Official Mahatma Gandhi eArchive, http://www.mahatma.org.in/quotes/quotes.jsp?link=qt.

2. Claudia H. Deutsch, "New Surveys Show That Big Business Has a P.R. Problem," *New York Times,* December 9, 2005.

3. John Harwood, "The *Wall Street Journal / NBC News* Poll—Washington Wire: A Special Weekly Report From *Wall Street Journal's* Capital Bureau," *Wall Street Journal,* January 21, 2005.

4. Ronald Alsop, "Ranking Corporate Reputations—Tech Companies Score High in Yearly Survey as Google Makes Its Debut in Third Place; Autos, Airlines, Pharmaceuticals Lose Ground," *Wall Street Journal,* December 6, 2005.

5. http://www.ifpma.org/News/InTheMedia.aspx. December 8, 2005 "New IFPMA survey highlights major contributions . . ."

6. Tom Wright, "The Pharmaceutical Horizon Beckons," *New York Times,* August 13, 2005.

7. Robert D. Hormats, in discussion with the author, July 2005.

8. Robert D. Hormats, "Purpose and Principles for America in the 21st Century," Precommencement Address for the NYU Stern School of Business, May 11, 2005.

9. Steven Perlstein, "Pillars of Corporate Kindness," *Washington Post,* December 24, 2003.

10. Gareth Chadwick, "Sustainable Development: Profit with a Conscience," *Independent* (United Kingdom), March 21, 2005.

11. Kathy Bloomgarden, Precommencement address to IMD, MBA Graduates, September 2004.

12. Ronald Alsop, "Career Journal—M.B.A. Track: Recruiters Seek M.B.A.s Trained In Responsibility," *Wall Street Journal*, December 13, 2005.

13. Jennifer Heldt Powell, "Nestlé Chief Rejects the Need to 'Give Back' to Communities," *Boston Herald*, March 9, 2005.

14. Joel Bakan, *The Corporation: The Pathological Pursuit of Profit and Power* (New York: Free Press, 2004), 36.

15. M. Friedman, "The Social Responsibility of Business Is to Increase Its Profits, *New York Times Magazine*, September 13, 1970; see also M. Friedman, "The Social Responsibility of Business," in T. L. Beauchamp and N. E. Bowie, eds., *Ethical Theory and Business* Engelwood Cliffs, N.J.: Prentice-Hall, 1983), pp. 81–83.

16. "Mastering Corporate Governance," *Financial Times Supplement*, June 3, 2005.

17. White paper prepared by MBA students for Sustainable Enterprise class taught by Professors Albert H. Segars and James H. Johnson. Kenan-Flagler Business School, University of North Carolina, 2004. Available online at www.cse.unc.edu.

18. Grahame F. Thompson, "Global Corporate Citizenship," *Competition and Change* 9, no. 2 (June 2005): 131–52.

19. p. 20, http://www.sustainability-index.com/djsi_pdf/news/MonthlyUpdates/DJSI_Update_0510.pdf

20. Novartis International AG, Mission Statement, http://www.novartis.com/about_novartis/en/our_mission.shtml.

21. Daniel Vasella, (remarks at the Annual Novartis Management Meeting, Interlaken, Switzerland) January 2001.

22. Ibid.

23. John Quelch and V. Kasturi Rangan, "Profit Globally, Give Globally," *Harvard Business Review*, December 1, 2003.

24. Floyd Norris, "Business Ethics and Other Oxymorons," *New York Times*, April 20, 2003.

25. Daniel Vasella, "Improving Third World Health," *Chief Executive*, December 2004.

26. http://www.novartis.com/corporate_citizenship/en/02_2003_code_of_conduct.shtml

27. Natural Marketing Institute.

28. Ian Davis, "The Biggest Contract," *Economist*, May 28, 2005.

29. Daniel Vasella, Speech at the American Swiss Foundation, November 17, 2004.

30. Ibid.

31. Daniel Vasella, M.D. with Robert Slater, *Magic Cancer Bullet: How a Tiny Orange Pill Is Rewriting Medical History* (New York: HarperBusiness, 2003), 13.

32. Vasella, in discussion with the author, August 2005.

33. Ibid.

34. Ibid.

35. Ibid.

36. David Kirkpatrick, "Chipping Away at Intel: CEO Hector Ruiz Came From Humble Roots to Propel AMD into the Big Leagues," *Fortune*, November 1, 2004.

37. Jonathan Kirn, "Bringing the Internet to the Whole World," *Washington Post*, April 29, 2005.

38. Alan Murray, "Citicorp CEO Pursues a Culture of Ethics," *Wall Street Journal*, March 2, 2005.

39. Mitchell Pacelle, Martin Fackler, and Andrew Morse, "Mission Control," *Wall Street Journal*, December 22, 2004.

40. Alan Murray, "Citicorp CEO Pursues a Culture of Ethics," *Wall Street Journal*, March 2, 2005.

41. Alex Brigham, "Exclusive Interview with Citigroup," http://welcome.corpedia.com.

42. Ibid.

43. Citigroup, "Corporate Initiatives, Corporate Governance and Business Practices," Spring 2005, http://www.citigroup.com/citigroup/citizen/data/initiatives05sp.pdf, 5, 8.

44. Jane Fuller, "Banking on a Good Reputation," *Financial Times*, June 21, 2003.

3: To Tell the Truth

1. Jenny Anderson, "Expelling the Ghost Of A.I.G. Past," *New York Times*, December 18, 2005.

2. Bloomberg News, "AIG's View of Regulators," *New York Times*, August 12, 2005.

3. *PR Newswire*, "New Organizational Communication Survey Reveals That Bosses Aren't Listening," June 28, 2005.

4. Donald V. Jernberg, "Whistle Blower Programs: The Counsel-Assisted Option," *Corporate Board*, September/October 2004: 7–11.

5. Ethics Resource Center, "Major Survey of America's Workers Finds Substantial Improvements in Ethics," http://www.ethics.org/releases/nr_20030521_nbes.html.

6. Daniel Ellsberg, a former government employee, made available to *The New York Times* documents from the Defense Department, popularly known as the Pentagon Papers, that contradicted much of what the U.S. government was telling the American people about the Vietnam War. The Justice Department obtained a court injunction prohibiting any further publication of the report by the *Times*, based on national security grounds. The U.S. Supreme Court overturned the injunction, citing the U.S. Constitution's guarantee of a free press.

7. Howard Kurtz, "New York Times Story Gives Texas Paper a Sense of Déjà Vu," WashingtonPost.com, April 30, 2003.

8. In 2003 Jessica Lynch, private first class in the United States Army, was held captive by Iraqi forces in a hospital in Nasiriya. With the aid of a local Iraq civilian, the U.S. military was able to locate and rescue Pfc. Lynch, making her the first American prisoner of war rescued since World War II, and the first woman ever.

9. Katharine Seelye, "Panel at the Times Proposes Steps to Increase Credibility," *New York Times*, May 9, 2005.

10. Siegal Committee, The Siegal Committee Report, July 28, 2003, 7, http://www.nytco.com/pdf/committeereport.pdf.

11. Jack Welch and Suzy Welch, *Winning* (New York: Harper Business, 2005), 25–31.

12. Siegal Committee, The Siegal Committee Report, 16 and 32.

13. Ibid., 51.

14. James C. Moore, "Not Fit to Print," Salon.com, May 27, 2004; Charles Layton, "Miller Brohaha," *American Journalism Review*, Aug./Sept. 2003.

15. Editors, "The Times and Iraq," *New York Times*, May 26, 2004.

16. Mark Jurkowitz, "Press Takes a Hard Look Within After Scandal Editors Vow to Work More Diligently for Readers' Trust," *Boston Globe*, May 28, 2003.

17. Michael Mayo, "Finding the Right Balance While Striking a Chord," SunSentinel.com, July 31, 2005.

18. "I Survived—I Survived—Tony Blair's Survival," *Economist*, January 31, 2004.

19. Value Alliance Company, "Accounting and Control Issues," *Corporate Governance Alliance Digest,* May 13, 2004.

20. Chip Cummins, Susan Warren, Alexei Barrionuevo, and Bhushan Bahree, "Losing Reserve: At Shell, Strategy and Structure Fueled Troubles— Oil Giant Relied on Its Prowess for Finding Fresh Oil—and Fell Behind Rivals—Dual Boards and Multiple Fiefs," *Wall Street Journal,* March 12, 2004.

21. "Royal Dutch/Shell to Be Unified July 20," Dow Jones International News, May 19, 2005.

22. Ibid.

23. Heather Won Tesoriero, Ilan Brat, Gary McWilliams, and Barbara Martinez, "Side Effects: Merck Loss Jolts Drug Giant, Industry—In Landmark Vioxx Case, Jury Tuned Out Science, Explored Cover-up Angle—'Shadow' Panel at McDonald's," *Wall Street Journal,* August 22, 2005.

24. Ibid.

25. John Simons, "More Woes at Merck ; The Stock's Down; the Pipeline's Dry. Is It Time For a Change at the Top?" *Fortune,* December 8, 2003.

26. Carol Hymowitz, "Management Missteps in '04," *Wall Street Journal,* December 21, 2004.

27. Ibid.

28. James B. Stewart, "Common Sense: First Vioxx Verdict Casts Doubt on Merck, But Not the Industry," *Wall Street Journal,* August 24, 2005.

29. Alex Berenson, "Side Effects May Include Heartburn," *New York Times,* May 21, 2005.

30. Roger Parloff, "The Preacher Who's Raising Hell with Merck," *Fortune,* August 8, 2005.

31. Alex Berenson, "Jury Calls Merck Liable in Death of Man on Vioxx," *New York Times,* August 22, 2005.

32. Min Wu (New York University Stern School of Business), "Earnings Restatements, 1997–2Q2005," [Chart], 2005, http://ihome.ust.hk/~acwu.

33. Rosabeth Moss Kantar, *Confidence* (New York: Random House, 2004), 81.

34. Duane Windsor, in discussion with Nancy Shepherdson, September 2005.

4: Seizing Opportunity from Disaster

1. Ed Breen, in discussion with the author, July 2005.
2. Jyoti Thottam, "Can This Man Save Tyco?" *Time*, February 9, 2004.
3. See note 2.
4. Claudia H. Deutsch, "As Ex-Bosses Await Their Fate, Tyco Stages a Come-back," *New York Times*, March 22, 2004.
5. Robert Hormats, in discussion with the author, July 2005.
6. Susquehanna Financial Group, June 16, 2005.
7. Christine Tierney, "Renault Awaits New CEO After Remarkable Era of Schweitzer, *Detroit News*, April 19, 2005.
8. Carlos Ghosn, "Saving the Business Without Losing the Company," *Harvard Business Review* 37 (January 1, 2002): 6.
9. Ibid.
10. Eric Pillmore, in discussion with Nancy Shepherdson February 2006.
11. Ibid.
12. Welch and Welch, *Winning*, 251.
13. David Lei and John W. Slocum Jr., "Strategic and Organizational Requirements for Competitive Advantage," *Academy of Management Executive* 19, no. 1 (2005), 38.
14. "Deloitte: A Firm in Full," interview with Paul Robinson, February 16, 2006, *Consulting Magazine*, July/August 2004.
15. Ibid.
16. Claudia Deutsch, *New York Times*, March 22, 2005.
17. Ed Breen in discussion with the author, July 2005.
18. Andrew S. Grove, *Only the Paranoid Survive* (New York: Random House, 1999), p 26.

5: Love Thy Enemy: The Benefits of Taking Critics Inside

1. Henry David Thoreau, *Quotations*.
2. "Mr. Energy," *World Link* 12, no. 5 (October/November 1999): 16.
3. Nick Butler, in discussion with the author, December 2005.
4. *Charlie Rose Show*, October 6, 2005.
5. Ibid.
6. Darcy Frey, "How Green Is BP?" *New York Times*, December 8, 2002.
7. Bhushan Bahree et al., "BP Won't Abandon Driving Force," *Wall Street Journal Europe*, November 15, 2003.

8. Alyson Ward, "Purchase with a Purpose," Star-Telegram.com, April 24, 2005.

9. "100 Best Corporate Citizens for 2005," www.business-ethics.com/whats_new/100best.html.

10. Natural Marketing Institute.

11. "About Us" and "Our Mission and Goals," www.idealswork.org.

12. Jack Neff, "Christian Group Spooks Advertisers," AdAge.com, October 25, 2004.

13. Sandra Waddock (professor of management in the Carroll School of Management, Boston College), in discussion with Nancy Shepherdson, June 14, 2005; and Sandra Waddock et al., "Responsibility: The New Business Imperative," Academy of Management Executive, May 2002, 27.

14. Steve Stecklow, "Virtual Battle: How a Global Web of Activists . . . ," *Wall Street Journal,* June 7, 2005.

15. Sandra Waddock (professor of management in the Carroll School of Management, Boston College), in discussion with Nancy Shepherdson, June 14, 2005; and Sandra Waddock et al., "Responsibility: The New Business Imperative," *Academy of Management Executive,* May 2002, 27.

16. "Environmental History Timeline," www.radford.edu/~wkovarik/envhist/11nineties.html.

17. Andrew Davidson, "The Andrew Davidson Interview: John Browne," *Management Today,* December, 1999, 60–65.

18. "Green Audit Puts BP Amoco in Pollution Reduction Lead," *Petroleum Economist* 66, no. 7 (July, 1999): 35.

19. Janet Guyon, "A Big-Oil Man Gets Religion," *Fortune,* March 6, 2000.

20. Fiona Harvey, "A Good Name Can Pay Big Dividends," *Financial Times* Report: World's Most Respected Companies, *Financial Times,* November 19, 2004.

21. Nick Butler, in discussion with the author, December 2005.

22. Ibid.

23. See note 2 above.

24. Lee Edwards, in discussion with the author, October 2005.

25. Ibid.

26. Ibid.

27. Kevin Coughlin, "To Bury a Gas: Shots in the Dark," *Star-Ledger,* March 6, 2005.

28. "Majors Accept Green Fate," *Petroleum Economist* August 2002, 28.

29. www.bp.com.

30. Ibid.
31. Smoking & Health Issues: Cigarette Smoking and Disease http://www
    .philipmorrisusa.com.
32. Andy Serwerk et al., "Bruised in Bentonville," *Fortune*, April 18, 2005,
    84.
33. "The Everyday Price Cutter: Face Value," *Economist*, September 11,
    2004, 372.
34. Nancy Cleeland and Debora Vrana, "Wal-Mart CEO Takes Case to Cali-
    fornia," *Los Angeles Times*, February 24, 2005.
35. Michael Barbaro, "Wal-Mart Rebuts Its Critics; Company Launches Ma-
    jor Media Campaign to Improve Its Image," *Washington Post*, January
    14, 2005.
36. Stephanie Strom, "Wal-Mart Donates $35 Million for Conservation,"
    New York Times, April 14, 2005.
37. Mark A. Stein, "Some Corporate Scandals Near Partial Resolutions,"
    New York Times, December 31, 2005.
38. Simon Zadek, "The Path to Corporate Responsibility," *Harvard Business
    Review* (December 2004), 125–32.
39. http://www.cleanclothes.org/faq/faq03.htm.
40. Clean Clothes Campaign, "An Open Letter to Phillip Knight, CEO of
    Nike, Inc.," www.cleanclothes.org/companies/nike-99-9-2.html.
41. Ibid.
42. Meg Carter, "Ethical Business Practices Come into Fashion," *Financial
    Times*, April 19, 2005.
43. Mark Gunther, "The Mosquito in the Tent," *Fortune*, May 31, 2004.
44. Matthew Yeomans, "Banks Go for Green," *Time*, May 30, 2005.
45. Ronald J. Alsop, "Corporate Reputation: Anything But Superficial—The
    Deep but Fragile Nature of Corporate Reputation," *Journal of Business
    Strategy* 25, no. 6: 21–29.
46. Jeffrey O'Connell, "A Proposed Remedy for Medical Malpractice Mis-
    eries," 51st Annual Meeting of the American College of Obstetricians
    and Gynecologists, April 28, 2003, http://cgood.org/healthcare-
    reading-cgpubs-speeches-10.html.

6: Courageous Realism Conquers Wishful Thinking

1. Fred Hassan, in discussion with the author, August 2005.
2. Ann Tenbrunsel, in discussion with Nancy Shepherdson, June 2005.

3. "Carly Fiorina Resigns as Hewlett-Packard CEO, Chairman," *Dow Jones Business News*, February 9, 2005.

4. Gardiner Harris, "Schering-Plough Is Hurt by Plummeting Pill Costs," *New York Times*, July 8, 2003.

5. Robert Langreth, "Back From the Morgue," *Forbes Global*, December 8, 2003.

6. "SP Sees No Need for Merger with Another Firm," *Wall Street Journal*, June 28, 1999.

7. Robert Langreth, "SP CEO Kogan Damps Talk of Merger, Is Named Chairman," *Wall Street Journal*, September 9, 1998.

8. Ibid.

9. Gardiner Harris, "Guilty Plea Seen for Drug Maker," *New York Times*, July 16, 2004.

10. Melody Petersen, "Drug Maker to Pay $500 Million Fine for Factory Lapses," *New York Times*, May 18, 2002.

11. Melody Petersen, "At Schering, Optimism and Problems," *New York Times*, January 15, 2002.

12. David Schwab, "SP Talks Products, Not Problems," *Star-Ledger*, June 29, 2001.

13. Reuters, "Schering-Plough Lowers Profit Forecast Substantially," *New York Times*, December 5, 2002.

14. Geoff Dyer and Adrian Michaels, "SEC Fines Schering $1 M," *Financial Times*, September 10, 2003.

15. Jeff Smith and David Milstead, "An Unbalanced Sheet; SEC Lays Out How Nacchio May Have Cooked Qwest Books," *Rocky Mountain News*, March 19, 2005.

16. According to the SEC, the September 2000 acquisition of the telco Genuity added $100 million in revenue and $80 million in profit to Qwest's third quarter results, but only because management structured the deal improperly in order to book the sales and profits immediately (David Milstead, "Execs Tweaked Deals to Meet Revenue Goals, SEC Alleges" *Rocky Mountain News*, February 26, 2003).

17. David Futrelle, "Qwest: Don't Hang Up Yet; Wall Street May Not Like the Embattled Telecom, but Some Investors See an Opportunity," *Money Magazine*, April 1, 2002.

18. Kris Hudson, "Nacchio an Icon of Guts, Hubtis," Denver Post, March 16, 2005.

19. Mark Gimein, "What Did Joe Know?" *Fortune*, May 12, 2003.

20. Patricia Sellers, "The New Breed; The Latest Crop of CEOs Is Disciplined, Deferential, Even a Bit Dull. What a Relief," *Fortune*, November 18, 2002.
21. Jon Van, "Next Goal for Once-Struggling Qwest: Profit in 2006," *Chicago Tribune*, February 15, 2006.
22. Fred Hassan, in discussion with the author, August 2005.
23. Ibid.
24. Ibid.
25. Ibid.
26. Ibid.
27. Christopher Bowe, "Hassan Faces Toughest Drug Test," *Financial Times*, October 22, 2003.
28. Ibid.
29. Ibid.
30. Ibid.
31. Ibid.
32. http://www.kenlayinfo.com.
33. John Knapp, in discussion with Nancy Shepherdson, June 2005.

7: Riding the Technology Wave

1. Thomas L. Friedman, *The Lexus and the Olive Tree* (New York: Anchor Books, 1999), 199.
2. World Economic Forum/Gallup International Association, Voice of the People 2005, www.weforum.org.
3. Ibid.
4. John Thornhill, "The View of the Future from Davos World Economic Forum . . . ," *Financial Times*, January 31, 2006.
5. William I. Huyett and S. Patrick Viguerie, "Extreme Competition," *McKinsey Quarterly* 1 (2005): 47.
6. Jonathan Schwartz, Jonathan's Blog, December 9, 2005, http://blogs.sun.com/roller/page/jonathan/20051209.
7. Kevin Allison, "The iPod Halo Is Apple's Great Hope . . . ," *Financial Times*, January 9, 2006.
8. James Nelson, "Clayton Christensen: Think New to Act New," *New Zealand Management*, May 1, 2005.
9. Clayton M. Christensen, *The Innovator's Dilemma* (New York: HarperBusiness Essentials, 2003), 165.

10. Clay Christensen, in discussion with Nancy Shepherdson, January 2006.

11. Richard Levine, World Economic Forum, 2006, Open Systems of Innovation panel, pers. comm.

12. "The Best and Worst Managers of 2004—The Best Managers: Anne Mulcahy; Xerox," *Business Week*, January 10, 2005.

13. Anne Mulcahy's Comments for Third Quarter 2000 Earnings Pre-Announcement (as delivered), 8:30 A.M., October 3, 2000.

14. Daniel Eisenberg, "An Image Problem At Xerox with Competitors . . . ," *Time*, Oct. 30, 2000.

15. Olga Kharif, "Anne Mulcahy Has Xerox by the Horns," http://www.businessweek.com/, May 23, 2003.

16. Ibid.

17. Carol Hymowitz, "Should CEOs Tell the Truth About Being in Trouble," *Wall Street Journal*, February 15, 2005.

18. Chris Warren, "Change Your Language," *American Way*, March 1, 2003: 63–65.

19. Patricia Riley (director of the Annenberg Research Network on Globalization and Communication at the University of Southern California), in discussion with Nancy Shepherdson, February 2006.

20. Scott McNealy, "Share the Crown Jewels to Create New Markets," *Financial Times*, February 16, 2006.

21. Jonathan Schwartz, Jonathan's Blog, January 5, 2005, http://blogs.sun.com/roller/page/jonathan?/entry=developers_don_t_buy_things.

22. Scott McNealy, editorial, "Share the Crown Jewels and Create New Markets," *Financial Times*, February 16, 2006.

23. See note 4 above.

24. Dan Scheinman, in discussion with the author, February 2006.

25. Ibid.

26. Matt Richtel and Ken Belson, "Acquisition Offers Hint of Cisco's Strategy," *New York Times*, November 19, 2005.

27. Richard Foster and Sarah Kaplan, *Creative Destruction* (New York: Currency, 2001), 63.

28. Bill Alpert, "On the Ball: IBM Finds its Balance—Just as Businesses May Boost Tech Spending," *Barron's*, November 10, 2003.

29. Paul McDougall, "IBM's Future Is in Business-Performance Transformation," *Information Week*, January 10, 2005, www.informationweek.com/story/showArticle.jhtml?articleID=56900493.

30. Ibid.

31. Daniel Lyons, "Dancing Lessons: Some of IBM's Biggest Customers Are Pulling the Plug," *Forbes*, March 14, 2005.

32. Samuel J. Palmisano, Paul Hemp, and Thomas A. Stewart, "Leading Change When Business Is Good: The HBR Interview—Samuel J. Palmisano," *Harvard Business Review* (December 1, 2004): 60.

33. Ibid.

34. David Orgel, "7-Eleven's Extreme Makeover: Fresh-Foods Edition," *Supermarket News*, September 20, 2004.

35. Jim Keyes, in discussion with Nancy Shepherdson, February 2006.

36. "7-Eleven Strategies for Success," *Convenience Store News*, March 24, 2005.

37. Robert Vosburgh, "7-Exchange Rates Highly," *Supermarket News*, March 14, 2005.

38. Mark Gottfredson, Rudy Puryear, and Stephen Phillips, "Strategic Sourcing: From Periphery to the Core," *Harvard Business Review* (February 1, 2005):132.

39. Jim Keyes, in discussion with Nancy Shepherdson, February 2006.

40. Rosabeth Moss Kantar, *Confidence* (New York: Random House, 2004), 81.

8: Engage in the Public Policy Game

1. www.brainyquote.com/quotes/quotes/j/johnfkenn132358.

2. Nicholas D. Kristof, "Take a Hike," *New York Times*, January 31, 2006.

3. "The McKinsey Global Survey of Business Executives : Business and Society—Web Exclusive," *McKinsey Quarterly*, January 2006, www.McKinseyquarterly.com.

4. Alison Maitland, "The Frustrated Will to Act for Public Good . . . ," *Financial Times*, January 25, 2006.

5. Douglas A. Schuler (associate professor of management, Rice University, Jesse Jones Graduate School of Management), interview with Nancy Shepherdson, September 12, 2005.

6. Suzanne Vranica, "Gerber Pushes Parents to Feed Healthier Diet to Their Babies," *Wall Street Journal*, August 19, 2002.

7. Kurt Schmidt, in discussion with the author, July 2006.

8. Kristof, "Take a Hike."

9. Michael D. Lord, "Constituency Building As the Foundation for Corporate Political Strategy," *Academy of Management Executive* 17, no. 1 (February 2003): 112–24.

10. Carl Johnson, in discussion with the author, April 2006.

11. George Parker and John Mason, "EU Legal Threat to Junk Food Advertising," *Financial Times*, January 19, 2005.

12. Floyd Norris, "Off the Charts: Business Casting the First Stone," *International Herald Tribune*, January 27, 2006.

13. Alison Leigh Cowan, "Hartford House Votes to Limit School Junk Food Sales," *New York Times*, May 19, 2005.

14. Melanie Warner, "Guidelines Are Urged in Food Ads for Children," *New York Times*, March 17, 2005.

15. J.-P. Bonardi, A. Hillman, G. Keim, "The Attractiveness of Political Markets: Implications for Firm Strategy." *Academy of Management Review*, http://www.ivey.uwo.ca/faculty/jpbonardi/AMR-FinalVersion-April2003.pdf, April 6, 2003.

16. Andrew Ward, "A Better Model? Diversified Pepsi Steals Some of Coke's Sparkle," *Financial Times*, February 28, 2005.

17. Chad Terhune, "Industry News: Pepsi Outlines Ad Campaign for Healthy Food," *Wall Street Journal*, October 15, 2005.

18. Statement by Steve Reinemund, chairman and chief executive officer of PepsiCo, taken from the company's 2004 annual report.

19. Coca-Cola, Make Every Drop Count Campaign, http://www2.coca-cola.com/makeeverydropcount/our_commitment.html

20. Ibid.

21. John Griffiths, "Help the Environment and the Bottom Line As Well," *Financial Times*, March 30, 2005; and Richard J. Newman, "Invasion of the Green Machines," *U.S. News and World Report*, May 9, 2005.

22. Chang-Ran Kim, "Rivals Turn Up Heat to Challenge Toyota Hybrid Push," Reuters, January 11, 2006.

23. Associated Press, "Hybrids to be a Major Part of Toyota's Future," http://www.msnbc.msn.com/id/8813226/, August 3, 2005.

24. John Griffiths, "Help the Environment and the Bottom Line As Well . . . ," *Financial Times*, March 30, 2005.

25. Keith Naughton et al., "Toyota Triumphs," *Newsweek International*, May 9, 2005.

26. Ibid.

27. David Ignatius, "Corporate Green," *Washington Post*, May 11, 2005.

28. Jeff Immelt, "Global Environmental Challenges." Speech, George Washington School of Business, Washington, D.C., May 9, 2005.

29. Ibid.

30. Doug Schuler, in discussion with Nancy Shepherdson, 2005.

31. Joshua Kurlantzick, "Serving Up Success," *Entrepreneur,* November 1, 2003, www.entrepreneur.com; and Jeanne Cummings, "Legislative Grind," *Wall Street Journal,* April 12, 2005.

32. Van Yeutter, interview with author, Cargill, March 8, 2006.

33. Marc Gunther, "Cops of the Global Village," *Fortune,* June 27, 2005.

34. Armando Garcia, in discussion with Nancy Shepherdson, 2005.

35. Floyd Norris, "Off the Charts: Business Casting the First Stone," *International Herald Tribune,* January 27, 2005.

36. Michael D. Lord, "Constituency Building As the Foundation for Corporate Political Strategy," *Academy of Management Exec.* 17.1 (February 2003), 112–124.

9: Respecting Culture in the Drive for Performance

1. In George A. Panichas, Kafka's Afflicted Vision: A Literary Theological Critique, *Humanitas* 17, nos. 1 and 2 (2004).

2. William Meyers, "Conscience in a Cup of Coffee," *U.S. News and World Report,* October 31, 2005, 48–50.

3. Patrick J. Kiger, "Corporate Crunch," *Workforce Management,* April 2005, 34; and Mitchell Lee Marks and Phillip H. Mirvis, "Managing Mergers, Acquisitions, and Alliances: Creating an Effective Transition Structure," *Organizational Dynamics* 3 (2000): 28.

4. William Holstein, "A Soft Touch That Unleashed Motorola's Potential . . . ," *Financial Times,* February 27, 2006.

5. Ibid.

6. Donna McAleese and Owen Hargie, "Five Guiding Principles of Culture Management: A Synthesis of Best Practice," *Journal of Communication Management* 9, no. 2 (2004): 155–70.

7. Andy Serwer, "Hot Starbucks to Go," *Fortune,* January 26, 2004.

8. Jeremy B. Dann, Howard Schultz, Debra Somberg, and Dan Levitan, "How To . . . Find a Hit as Big as Starbucks," *Business 2.0,* May 1, 2004.

9. "Starbucks Annual Meeting of Shareholders Starts Over a Cup of Coffee . . . ," *Business Wire,* www.businesswire.com, February 8, 2006.

10. Gretchen Weber, "Preserving the Counter Culture," *Workforce Management*, February 2005, 34.

11. See note 9 above.

12. Q1 2006 Starbucks Earnings Conference Call, February 1, 2006, http:// retail.seekingalpha.com/article/6446/

13. See note 9 above.

14. Barbara Kiviat, "Selling Latte to the Masses," *Time*, April 26, 2004.

15. See note 12 above.

16. Geoffrey A. Fowler, "Storm in a Coffee Cup," *Far Eastern Economic Review*, April 22, 2004, 58.

17. See note 10 above.

18. Carol Hymowitz, "Two Giants, Two Images," *Wall Street Journal Europe*, December 12, 2005.

19. William Meyers, "Conscience in a Cup of Coffee."

20. Chris Speechley, "The Changing Nature of Leadership," *Measuring Business Excellence* 9, no.1 (2005): 3, 5.

21. Nitin Nohria, William Joyce, and Bruce Roberson, "What Really Works," *Harvard Business Review*, July 1, 2003, 4.

22. Maija Pesola and Simon London, "Deal to Create Titan Beset by Ill Feeling," *Financial Times*, February 10, 2005.

23. Hewlett-Packard Timeline, www.hp.com/hpinfo/abouthp/histnfacts/timeline/hist_70s.html.

24. Bill Saporito et al., "Why Carly's Out . . . ," *Time*, February 21, 2005.

25. Bill Breen, "The Big Score," 65.

26. Carly Fiorina, James Gillies Alumni Lecture, Schulich School of Business, York University, Toronto, October 28, 2003, www.hp.com/hpinfo/execteam/speeches/fiorina.schulich.html.

27. Gary Rivlin and John Markoff, "Tossing Out a Chief Executive," *New York Times*, February 14, 2005.

28. John Markoff, "When+Adds Up to Minus, " *New York Times*, February 10, 2005.

29. Michael S. Malone, "What's the Hurd Instinct," *Wall Street Journal*, May 19, 2005.

30. Christopher Springmann, "The Best Job in the World," *Across the Board*, May/June 2003, 31–32.

31. Ben Elgin, "The Inside Story of Carly's Ouster," *Business Week*, February 21, 2005, 34; and Bill Breen, "The Big Score," *Fast Company*, September 1, 2003, 65.

32. Tom Krazit, "HP Taps NCR's Mark Hurd as New CEO," *PC World*, March 29, 2005.

33. George Binney, Gerhard Wilke, and Collin Williams, *Living Leadership: A*

Practical Guide for Ordinary Heroes (Harlow, England: Financial Times Prentice Hall, 2005), 7, 37.

34. Natasha Spring, "With His Eyes on the Prize," *Communication World*, Sept/Oct 2005, 28–29.

35. Aaron Ricadela, "HP Gets Practical," *Information Week*, April 4, 2005, 20.

36. Mark Hurd and Lars Nyberg, *The Value Factor: How Global Leaders Use Information for Growth and Competitive Advantage* (Princeton, N.J.: Bloomberg Press, 2004), 24.

37. Patrick J. Kiger, "Corporate Crunch", 28.

38. Ibid.

39. Daimler-Chrysler management in discussion with Nancy Shepherdson.

40. "The Mega-Media Business Model: Doomed to Fail, or Just Ahead of Its Time?" Research at Penn, July 31, 2002, www.upenn.edu/researchatpenn/article.php?309&Gus.

41. Michael A. Hiltzik and Sallie Hofmeister, "AOL Time Warner Propose Unprecedented Merger Worth $163 Billion," Washington Post/Los Angeles Times Wire Service, January 11, 2000.

42. See note 40 above.

43. TWX, Time Warner, Inc., chart and fundamentals reports, Fidelity.com.

44. John A. Byrne, "How to Lead Now," *Fast Company*, August 2003, 63.

45. Terry Bacon, "You Are How You Behave: Customers Can't Be Fooled," *Journal of Business Strategy* 25, no. 4 (2004): 37.

46. Alison Maitland, "Le Patron, der Chef, and the Boss," *Financial Times*, January 9, 2006.

47. "Apple Computers: The Rotten Core," *Economist*, July 11, 1998.

48. Joshua Hyatt, "The Real Secrets of Entrepreneurs," *Fortune*, November 15, 2004.

Conclusion: The Trust Imperative: A New Leadership Code

1. Michael Porter, Panel at the World Economic Forum, Davos, Switzerland 2006.

2. Jonathan Schwartz, Jonathan's Blog, December 9, 2005, http://blogs.sun.com/roller/page/jonathan/20051209.

3. Thomas Dougherty, *Directors' Handbook* (Skadden Arps, 2001), p. 203.

4. Thomas Donaldson, "Defining the Value of Doing Good Business," *Financial Times*, June 2, 2005.

About the Author

Kathy Bloomgarden is Co-CEO of Ruder Finn, Inc., one of the world's largest and most successful global public relations agencies. As a recognized communications advisor and confidante to some of today's most influential corporate leaders, Dr. Bloomgarden shapes communications programs that help executive teams effectively establish trust with their employees, their customers, the business community and society at large.

Dr. Bloomgarden is a member of The Council on Foreign Relations, Women's Leadership Board of Harvard University's John F. Kennedy School of Government, and the board of the Foundation for National Institutes of Health. She frequently represents the communications industry perspective at world events such as the World Economic Forum Annual Conference in Davos and Fortune Magazine's CEO summits, Most Powerful Women Summit, and Aspen Institute Brainstorm Events. She graduated with a B.A. from Brown University, and has an M.A. and a Ph.D. from Columbia University in Political Science, as well as a certificate from the East Asian Institute. She is fluent in French, and has a working knowledge of Chinese, Italian, German, and Russian.

Dr. Bloomgarden is married, with three children.